THE BELIEVER'S GUIDE TO
SPIRITUAL WARFARE

The Believer's Guide to Spiritual Warfare

Thomas B. White

Servant Publications
Ann Arbor, Michigan

Vine Books is an imprint of Servant Publications especially
designed to serve Evangelical Christians.

The Bible texts in this publication are from *The Holy Bible, New
International Version* copyright © 1973, 1978, 1984 International
Bible Society. Used by permission of Zondervan Bible Publishers.

Published by Servant Publications
P.O. Box 8617
Ann Arbor, Michigan 48107

Cover design by Michael Andaloro
Cover illustration by Martin Soo Hoo

98 99   18 17 16 15

Printed in the United States of America
ISBN 0-89283-680-6

Library of Congress Cataloging-in-Publication Data

White, Thomas B., 1947-
   The believer's guide to spiritual warfare : wising up to Satan's
influence in your world / Thomas B. White.
      p. cm.
   Includes bibliographical references.
   ISBN 0-89283-680-6
   1. Demonology.   2. Occultism—Religious aspects—
Christianity—Controversial literature.   3. Spiritual life—Baptist
authors.   I. Title.   II. Title: Spiritual warfare.
BT975.W47 1990
235′4—dc20   90-37964
                                                          CIP

Dedication

The labors that have gone into this book,
and any fruit that emerges from it,
are dedicated to Paul W. Dekker,
a gentle giant of a man
who fathered and befriended me
in the early days of my spiritual formation
in San Diego, California.

Paul patiently provided fertilizer for my young tree,
enabling me to grow in grace,
sharpen my discernment,
and learn the way of Jesus' love.

Contents

Preface

I AM A GRADUATE OF THE ILL-FAMED high school class of 1965. If ever there was a period of American history that could be explained in terms of spiritual warfare, the mid-1960s qualifies. More was happening during those years than meets the analytical eyes of sociologists and political scientists. Social violence, an unwinnable foreign war, a radical shift in values, and an influx of philosophies and gurus from the East entered our culture through the music and media of the youth subculture. Alongside these social dynamics strange spiritual forces were at work. Unseen forces aggressively attempted to divert our culture from the moorings of our Judeo-Christian heritage.

New openness to the teachings of spiritualism, astrology, Zen Buddhism, and Hinduism prepared the way for the current popularity of New Age religions and practices. A line from one popular song conjured up images of the shift in the collective consciousness: "This is the Dawning of the Age of Aquarius." It was apparent to me then, and it is clearer to me now, that there indeed *were* invisible spiritual forces at work.

During the early 1960s, growing up in the suburbs of Rochester, New York, I had a very disillusioning experience with organized Christianity. After logging three years of college, I began a personal quest for truth. I sought out spiritualists in New York City, a Tibetan Buddhist monk in Vermont, and Baba Ram Dass in

Boston (formerly Richard Alpert, Timothy Leary's Harvard associate). In 1968 I came in contact with writings dictated by an "ascended master" that offered an extensive blueprint for the coming of the New Age. The author spoke of the plan to place proponents of the New Consciousness at high levels of government, economic, and educational institutions in preparation for worldwide political and religious unity. At that time, the oneness of all world religions and the growth of a global community seemed lofty goals.

Through these many exposures, I experienced threatening times when a real and personal power of deception seemed tangible to me. The spiritual realm was as real to me as down-to-earth daily life. With a measure of ignorance mixed with youthful folly, I pushed open doors to the supernatural. Yet in every encounter, I had the sense of predestined protection surrounding and sustaining me, drawing me forward to a point of light. That point finally came at the end of a long, desperate journey from Kennebunkport, Maine to Bellingham, Washington.

In October 1969, I met Harlie Goodwin, a former pastor. He listened to me, loved me, and gently led me to the Savior in his living room. Staring up at the stars in Harlie's apple orchard, I made an agreement with my newfound Master: "Lord, the devil nearly destroyed my life. If you ever choose to use me to help others be free of his deception, I'll be available." At times in this ministry when I ponder the question, "Why would anyone choose to do *this*?" I remember that tender moment of conversion and the personal commitment I made to serve the King at any cost.

After graduating from Asbury Theological Seminary in 1975, I traveled and taught with Overseas Crusades, a mission committed to equipping the church and discipling nations. From 1977 to 1983, I was involved in local church ministry in Corvallis, Oregon. Then in 1983 the

Lord gave me the vision and faith to launch Mantle of Praise Ministries, which has now expanded to become Frontline Ministries. Our specialty is to equip both professional and lay workers to function with accurate and balanced discernment in the practice of spiritual authority. Our vision is to promote the practice of prayer that releases divine power and advances the kingdom of God. Much of this book has emerged from spiritual warfare seminars done for churches and Christian organizations. I hope to provide you with the insight and practical instruction necessary for living triumphantly in the days ahead.

I thank God for his special gifts to me. My wife Terri has been an unceasing source of encouragement, insight, and intercession for me and the ministry. We walk this path together. We are joyously indebted to Jerry and Sandra Kwast, who have been "on board" with us from the beginning. They have provided the ministry with an "upper room" for counseling, writing, and prayer. And we are grateful for the inestimable value of the persistent prayers of many who have shared this vision with us, and without whom this ministry could not have been sustained.

Introduction

At that time the kingdom of heaven will be like ten
virgins who took their lamps and went out to meet the
bridegroom. Five of them were foolish, and five were
wise. The foolish ones took their lamps but did not take
any oil with them. The wise, however, took oil in jars
along with their lamps.   Mt 25:1-4

IN OCTOBER OF 1989 I was preparing for a seminar in Minneapolis. The night before leaving, I didn't sleep very well. But just before the alarm went off at 3:45, I had a dream, a timely gift from the Spirit. I was boarding a school bus with other Christians, some familiar, some strangers. We were quiet and deliberate as we hurriedly entered the bus. Spontaneously, small groups came together in clusters and began to pray. The door closed, and the bus sped off into the streets of a large city, dodging cars and pedestrians at breakneck speed, yet with no threat of danger. We climbed a hill and came to a garbage dump. A hole opened in the midst of heaps of trash. The bus backed into the opening. As we backed in, I looked up to see an enormous stone cathedral, and suddenly we were surrounded by the presence of God. No one had to guess what we were there to do. We began to pray for the power of God's Spirit to orchestrate an awakening in the church, to strengthen its leaders, and to begin a worldwide harvest.

I do not claim this dream to be a vision or a revelation. It was a personal communique from God to me that was profoundly real and relevant, an affirmation of the priority of the hour—*this is a time to watch and pray.*

I feel called to pray with others for the awakening of the church and to take a strong stand against enemy resistance. The church has an opportunity to participate with the Lord in his mighty plans. He is raising an army anointed with spiritual authority to minister grace in the midst of the chaos of human sin. He builds a cathedral of prayer and praise right in the midst of man's folly.

At the Lausanne II Congress on World Evangelization in Manila in July 1989, the statement was made that for the first time in the history of the church we are consciously and corporately aware of a worldwide movement of prayer that is petitioning God for the release of his power to help us spread the gospel to every person on the globe. These are days of challenge. This is a season to watch and pray.

THE BIG PICTURE

Imagine Christ's agenda for the church prior to his second coming. No doubt he will purify his chosen to reflect his glory. He will surely test the fiber of our faith through trial. In the face of Satan's delusions, he might sovereignly restore supernatural grace and power to his people for a season of unprecedented revival and harvest. We might also expect to see a special anointing on our young people, a hunger for the deeper things of the Spirit.

I believe that God is preparing committed servants to meet the challenges of the 1990s. He is restoring the fullness of grace, gifts, wisdom, and authority required to face a foe who knows his time is short, and whose wrath is now being unleashed. One aspect of the Lord's agenda for the church is for his people to understand spiritual warfare—to learn to detect and deal with the subtleties of Satan.

Overtly, we face a flood of immorality, violence, and a vast array of behaviors destructive to human dignity. Covertly, we find seemingly endless psycho-spiritual groups that deny the gospel and deify humanity. And the "god of this world" promotes cultural values that glorify greed and idolize the pursuit of personal pleasure. What is the child of light to do? Too often the church is *re-active* in responding to this flood. But the role of the redeemed is to be courageously *pro-active* in devising and implementing strategies that penetrate and weaken the influence of evil.

Satan wants to divert people from Christ himself. Even now, he is motivated by the pride and jealousy that prompted his initial rebellion (Is 14:12-14; Ez 28:11-19). It is no mystery that at some point God will allow his adversary to construct a "powerful delusion" (2 Thes 2:11) accompanied with supernatural signs and wonders, designed to deceive and bring damnation to all who refuse to embrace the truth.

One modern example of Satan's work is the New Age movement, supposedly ushering in a new order of peace and harmony. In essence, the schemes of evil remain boringly the same. All that changes is the package. Knowledge, power, and self-deification were the very temptations of Eden.

Here is the challenge to the church: Those who are awake and alert in Christ, endowed with discernment and wisdom, must recognize that the arch-enemy of Christ is staging a strategic move to deceive and destroy people. The role of the redeemed is to wake up, sound a call to arms, and actively wage war against these schemes in the name and power of God. Our purpose is not to prevent the final manifestation of evil, as allowed by God. Our purpose is redemptive, to allow the Holy Spirit to wrench people free from the snares of Satan's deceptions.

HOW-TO'S OF HAND-TO-HAND COMBAT

When it comes to spiritual warfare, most Christians aren't concerned about the cosmic, but the hassles of daily life. We are concerned with issues related to our own spiritual survival, protection for our children, and finding God's power to deal with the needs and bondages of those around us. How do I receive the protection from the evil one promised by Jesus? How do I deal with a neighborhood friend who is dabbling with trance channeling? How do I pray for a child hooked on drugs? Do my prayers move God's hand in spiritual warfare? This is the sphere in which spiritual warfare is most relevant.

My goal in this book is to help Christians learn to pray more effectively and to equip them with tools to free themselves and others from enemy affliction. What we need are the how-to's of hand-to-hand combat: how to discern and deal with personal oppression; how to pray effectively for our families; how to sort out the demonic from emotional, psychological, and physical problems; how to release greater spiritual power in the face of evil; how to know when evil forces tamper with family life, with significant relationships, church life, ministry assignments, misdirected priorities, and devotional life. This dimension of kingdom life is not to be relegated to lone rangers working in para-church ministries. Resisting evil is a central aspect of gospel ministry for every believer and is intended to be practiced within the protective authority of the local church.

PRAYER OF CONSECRATION

Father, I thank you for the access I have to you through Jesus Christ, my High Priest. I choose in this moment to draw near to you. According to your promise, draw near to me. I acknowledge my need for greater grace. I ask you to touch my heart and fan into a flame the ember of love I have for you. Stir up the spark of commitment to your kingdom that already burns within. Father, give fresh light to my mind in understanding your truth. Give courage to my heart in following your ways.

Lord, I acknowledge my dependence upon you. Open the eyes of your servant to see as you see. Anoint my lips to speak as you would speak. Grant your servant the authority of your Son to stand against the evil one and his workers, and to speak triumph over them in Jesus' name. Impart to me your graces and gifts to fight and prevail in the battle for souls. Let nothing hinder the high and holy purposes you have for my life. Speak afresh to me. . . . I long to hear your voice. Train my hands for battle, and assign me my place in your army. Teach me the ways of your Spirit, and lead me in the path of understanding for Jesus' sake and for the cause of his kingdom. Amen.

ONE

A Reasoned, Seasoned Approach to Spiritual Warfare

Let those who love the LORD hate evil,
  for he guards the lives of his faithful ones
  and delivers them from the hand of the wicked.
Light is shed upon the righteous,
  and joy on the upright of heart. Ps 97:10

THROUGH THE YEARS, I HAVE BEEN CALLED on to exercise discernment and authority in dealing with real evil that touches real people. Over and over, people ask the same question: *How can you tell if a particular problem is caused by evil spirits?* After twenty years of counseling experience, I have decided it's better to be cautious, to avoid the temptation to attribute demonic activity to a problem.

Human nature has a certain fascination with super-natural evil. We can even hope that a particular struggle is demonic. If it is, perhaps spiritual surgery will take care of the problem, relieving us of responsibility for finding solutions to basic life problems. Only discernment and spiritual authority can reveal whether demonic activity is involved in a particular situation.

A LOOK AT THE LEVELS OF SPIRITUAL WARFARE

Cosmic Conflict. What exactly is spiritual warfare? Generally, there are *three distinct levels of warfare*. The first is the prehistoric and ongoing conflict between the Creator and his faithful angels on the one side, and the rebellious hierarchy of evil forces under Satan on the other. We can only speculate about the hand-to-hand combat presumed to occur at this level. The Bible does not say exactly how angels and demons do battle. Even so, Daniel 10 sheds some light on this warfare. The book of Job unveils a rather formal, defined type of interaction between Satan and God. As an adversary, an opponent of righteousness, God allows the devil a sanctioned latitude to do his dirty work of deceiving men and wreaking havoc on earth. However, he is held on a sovereign string, serving as a tempter and moral tester of men.

The Redeemed. The second level of the warfare is the battle between the demonic realm and the redeemed. Genesis 3:15, foundational for understanding spiritual conflict, provides a prophetic description of this battle in the judgment spoken against the serpent: "And I will put enmity between you and the woman, and between your offspring and hers; he will crush your head, and you will strike his heel." Hatred was to prevail between the sons of men and the seed of the serpent. And yet "he" (the deliverer who was to come, the Messiah) would deal the serpent a mortal blow, and himself receive a wound.

Jesus was wounded for our iniquities, yet these very wounds cleansed us of sin and crushed the powers of the evil one (Heb 2:14; 1 Jn 3:8). Until Jesus comes in glory with his angels to rid the universe of evil men and demons (2 Thes 1:5-10), the devil continues to "strike at the heel" of the body of Christ, lashing out at God by attacking the saints. This level of spiritual warfare is the tempting and trying, the taunting and haunting of men with the possibility and potency of evil. This level of the battle generally has two major dimensions. It is important here to see a distinction between a *direct* and an *indirect* struggle with supernatural evil.

To say that a Christian struggles with *direct* spiritual warfare is to describe some form of hand-to-hand combat, a tangible interference of intelligent evil beings with a child of God. This direct warfare is precisely what Paul describes so vividly in Ephesians 6 with the image of the soldier warding off "flaming arrows." Such warfare may involve enticement toward a specific sin, such as explosive anger or indulgence in pornography. Or it might manifest itself as doubt introduced into the mind of a believer who is weak in faith, or despondency undermining the fragile emotions of one who is wrestling with low self-esteem. In such cases, a real spirit is tangibly present and is committed to carrying out an assignment against a child of God. "Oppression" is the alien pressure that makes the normal challenges of life more difficult than they should be.

To say, on the other hand, that a Christian faces *indirect* spiritual warfare is to acknowledge that the devil and his forces exert a broad influence over the affairs of life, that indeed "the whole world is under the control of the evil one" (1 Jn 5:19). There is some glad news in the midst of the bad. Our adversary suffers a serious disadvantage: he is not omniscient, omnipotent, or omnipresent.

The focus of Satan's endeavors must be to invest his limited power where it will reap the greatest reward. His strategy, therefore, is to undermine values, promote godless ideologies and moral decay—anything that pollutes the minds and perverts the wills of people. Thus, communications media, school curricula, political and religious bodies, educational institutions, powerful leaders, each can become potential avenues of Satan's influence that touch the life of the believer. This is the predominant form of spiritual warfare we face. It is formidable and subtle. It has potential to seep into the lives of the best of us.

The Unredeemed. The third major level of spiritual warfare is to deceive and bind non-Christians. Paul tells us that "The god of this age has blinded the minds of unbelievers, so that they cannot see the light of the gospel of the glory of Christ, . . ." (2 Cor 4:4). Describing the Ephesian believers, he points out that they at one time were dead in sin and "followed the ways of this world and of the ruler of the kingdom of the air, the spirit who is now at work in those who are disobedient" (Eph 2:2). Disobedience to the gospel is promoted by the devil, who holds unbelievers in spiritual darkness and death. Jesus' commission to Paul thus makes sense: "to open their eyes and turn them from darkness to light, and from the power of Satan to God, so that they may receive forgiveness of sins . . ." (Acts 26:18).

In the conflicts between men, races, and nations, the greatest battle is the invisible wrestling match for the souls of men and women. This battle is the cutting edge of spiritual warfare. This is precisely why Jesus cautioned his disciples against an exuberant zeal concerning their authority over evil spirits. He urged them, instead, to remember "that your names are written in heaven" (Lk 10:20). No wonder front line evangelism is so tough. No wonder missionaries called to penetrate Islamic, Buddhist, or Hindu cultures labor with tears, trials, and testings. Having occupied cultural territories for generations, the enemy has a high interest in holding multitudes captive to his lies.

I may then venture the following definition: *Spiritual warfare is a multilevel conflict between good and evil initiated on the supernatural plane with the prehistoric rebellion of Lucifer, and transferred onto the natural plane with the fall of man. Satan, man's adversary, continues to work to deceive and divert people from salvation in Jesus Christ, and to harass and hinder Christians through enticement to sin and exploitation of weaknesses.* Because Satan is the author and initiator of original sin, and because he is the "god of this world," spiritual warfare involves a constant multidimensional battle against the world (system of ungodly values), the flesh (sin inherent to our humanity), and the devil (supernatural personification of evil). Warfare implies the likelihood of losses: eternal separation from God for the nonbeliever, and diminished effectiveness and suffering for the believer.

A DAY AT THE DUMP

The fall of creation was caused by sin. Sin was committed by man. And the sin of man was introduced by Satan, the originator of rebellion. Now, we live in physical bodies that are subject to the influence of sin. For example, each inherits genetic predispositions toward character traits as well as toward organic disorders and diseases. The consequences of choices we make, *e.g.,* career, marriage, financial investments, also have consequences for good or evil.

One purpose of discernment is to identify the *primary* cause of a particular problem. It is naive and simplistic to attribute most of life's hassles to the devil. Let me illustrate.

Several years back, I awoke on a crisp Saturday morning intending to celebrate the arrival of fall by taking my son out to the woods to cut and split firewood. The day before, I had purchased a used car, and we set out down the road. Within minutes, Joshua and I sat dazed on a rain-slick highway, recovering from a wreck, shaken, yet unharmed. As we surveyed the mashed metal and plastic, I couldn't easily shake that sick, depressive feeling that follows a life blooper: "Why wasn't I more careful? What a miserable way to start a day!"

We abandoned the car and hobbled home to report the minor tragedy to my wife. With inspired domestic insight, Terri suggested we redeem the day by clearing ten years of ancient relics and assorted refuse out of our attic. Terrific, I thought. After six hours of inhaling dust, wrestling with cobwebs, bashing and bruising my knees, and suffering that dreaded homeowner's disease, "insulation itch," we finally succeeded in ridding ourselves of a literal mountain of junk. Having carefully loaded everything onto a neighbor's trailer, I set off at 4:00 P.M. for the dump—the end of a difficult day was in sight.

The first sign of trouble came on Walnut Boulevard. I noticed a strange sound. I tilted my mirror to behold a large bamboo shade hanging from the bumper and dragging down the middle of the boulevard. I stopped and tied my load down a bit better, and headed up Highland Avenue for the open country. Suddenly, a familiar blue truck pulled alongside, and a friend shouted out to me, "You lost a mattress about a mile back!" In the middle of the highway, along with an old fry pan cover and an assortment of white, fluffy packing chips drifting in the breeze, sat the mattress. Exhausted, I pondered dragging the thing to the side of the road, lying down, and packing in the day.

I rolled into the dump at 4:50, just shy of closing time. With a slight surge of inner confidence that somehow all was now well, I backed up to the dump site—with a surprising jolt, the wheels of the trailer slipped off a concealed ledge and it sank down to the frame. As I began to unload, the darkened skies opened and drenched me with a downpour, seemingly timed just for me. I balanced my bones alongside the trailer and pondered my predicament: "Can this really be happening?" I climbed back in the car and gunned the engine—the wheels jumped free. Exulting in my deliverance, I raced to sweep out the trailer and make my getaway, only to hear the booming, angry voice of the dump cat operator, screaming at me from the hill above, "You can't dump there—you're in the wrong area!" Yes, I silently agreed. I am definitely in the wrong place. Wet and chagrined, I departed the dump, choosing as I wound my way home to follow the counsel of the psalmist:

> I will extol the LORD at all times;
> his praise will always be on my lips. Ps 34:1

Do you wonder, as I do, why we have days like that? Nothing really tragic happened, but hassle after hassle seemed to threaten my sanity. One thing I was sure of was that the Lord was testing my response and teaching me afresh to trust him. But could this have been a nasty spiritual assault, a flaming arrow aimed first at causing bodily harm in the accident, and then at crushing my spirit? Possibly. It is hard, even for a discerner of spirits, to know these things for sure. Experience tells me that the natural flow of life brings with it seasons of apparent chaos. Our quest to grow in the character of Christ calls us to face such times with grace. At the same time, such testings may be accompanied by supernatural attacks that seek to intensify and exploit our vulnerable moments. C.S. Lewis, a man wise in the ways of spiritual warfare, depicted a potent weapon in the Christian's arsenal: unconditional faith. Said the demon Screwtape to his apprentice nephew Wormwood:

Do not be deceived, Wormwood. Our cause is never more in danger than when a human, no longer desiring, but still intending to do our enemy's will, looks round upon a universe from which every trace of him seems to have vanished, and asks why he has been forsaken, and still obeys.[1]

I don't want to make you paranoid, but the Bible clearly tells us that we are surrounded by supernatural witnesses, demons and angels, interacting with our responses. We all have times of feeling that we have won or lost a battle, when more seems at stake than personal reputation. In any circumstance, we should ask, "Am I honoring the Lord with my response, or am I giving place to the devil's influence?"

SIN, SELF, AND SATAN

To sharpen our understanding of spiritual warfare, it helps to consider potential sources of the various problems people face. For example, if you are trying to understand a persistent pattern of violent anger, you might look at three possible sources: the natural *self* life of the person, the dynamic of *sin*, or the involvement of *Satan*.

First, the self life. This is the natural man, the human personality not yet controlled by the Spirit of Christ. It includes the reasoning, emotive, and volitional aspects of a person. Let's also include the physical body here, with its maze of biochemical interactions. An unbeliever functions on the level of the natural man, not yet aware of the things of God. The Christian who is born again receives the Holy Spirit. Paul thus exhorted the Ephesian believers to "put off your old self, which is being corrupted by its deceitful desires; to be made new in the attitude of your minds; and to put on the new self, created to be like God in true righteousness and holiness" (Eph 4:22-24).

The old way of thinking and doing, patterned by the natural man and his responses, is to be superseded by the new self, a fresh spiritual identity empowered by the Spirit. Paul's exhortation illustrates that even after giving our lives to Christ we deal with a mixture of old habits, thoughts, and temptations alongside our new life. And surely, the natural instincts of sexual drive, appetite, pain, and the biochemical processes of the body remain the same. What takes place in the Christian is a transformation from natural man to spiritual man. Any honest person will readily admit that sanctification involves time: we are all a people in process, dependent upon God's patience.

Second, there is the pervasive power of sin. Years ago, while studying at Asbury Theological Seminary, my Biblical Theology professor, Dr. Fred Layman, offered a definition of sin. I liked it so much, I wrote it down in the back of my study Bible:

> The principle of sin is not fundamentally some impulse, biological or psychological, which belongs essentially to fallen human nature, but rather is a spiritual dynamic, alien and distinct from human nature at the same time that it is immanently present within human nature. The operation and function of this spiritual dynamic are to enslave and condition the biological and psychological drives of human life in the service of sin.

Notice, sin is not an essential aspect of original human nature, but an alien force. Every Christian I have ever talked to identifies readily with Paul's transparency: "For what I want to do I do not do, but what I hate I do" (Rom 7:15). He goes on to say that in his "inner being" (the new man, longing to be like Christ) he delights in God's law, but in his body he experiences a contrary dynamic, the force of sin that seeks to dominate him by waging war in his mind (vs. 21-23). Sin in this context appears to be an *it*, a *thing* that clutches our lives and clamors constantly for attention.

Where did sin come from? From the personal pride and rebellion of Lucifer. Sin was then, and is now, willful violation of God's law. Because it is by definition personal in nature, it seems to have a life of its own. The "flesh" can be so strong that it appears to be demonic. A woman who battles with irrational jealousy, or a man who is addicted to pornography, feel that they can't control their impulses. Certainly Satan can take advantage of our sin as it operates in and through our human nature.

My point is that there are subtle, often indefinable lines that run between self, sin, and satanic influence. James illustrates this beautifully. Speaking of "bitter envy and selfish ambition" in the hearts of his readers, he states bluntly that "Such 'wisdom' does not come down from heaven but is earthly, unspiritual, of the devil" (Jas 3:15). He pinpoints all three elements of self, sin, and Satan in one inclusive description. It takes discernment to cut to the core of the problem. Such analysis dictates whether we exhort a brother or sister to submit to God, repent of sin, or resist Satan. In some cases, all three are in order. The church desperately needs Christians trained in discernment, able to undertake spiritual warfare that is guided both by Scripture and experience.

In the summer of 1987, I met with a small group of psychologists, psychiatrists, clergymen, and counselors for a "Symposium on the Spiritual and Psychological Dimensions of Evil." In the midst of a session, a participant lowered his glasses and caught the attention of everyone by uttering this profound statement: "The human person is a spiritual-psycho-socio-somatic being." An inspired, silent hush followed, as we pondered the breadth and depth of the observation. Man is a wondrous intermingling of divinely ordained ingredients. When faced with suffering of any sort, we must be aware that symptoms may be rooted in any one of a number of potential causes or combination of causes.

A BAPTISM OF FIRE

I am not trying to build a case against the existence of spiritual oppression. Unfortunately, it does exist and is all too real. In the spring of 1983, I was on the staff of a local church when I took a call from a fellow pastor serving a church in the mountains. Ted reported to me that he had recently led a fifty-year-old German tailor named Gerhard to the Lord. Instead of experiencing improvement, Gerhard was plunged into life-threatening battles with violent anger, depression, and suicidal impulses. I recall the drive up the mountain that April afternoon, thinking: "What am I getting into?" I met with Gerhard in his house trailer with his wife and Pastor Ted, five miles from town, with no phone, and no neighbor in sight.

I was spiritually rusty. It had been a while since I had dealt with the demonic. I wondered whether the limb I had crawled out onto was one of faith or foolishness. In the course of a brief interview, I learned that Gerhard had grown up in Berlin in the 1930s, and that his uncle and grandfather had been personally involved with Hitler. He went on to describe remembrances of strange meetings of government and military officials in his home. I mentioned that his struggle to walk with Christ might relate to spiritual forces connected with the darkness in his family. I suggested that we test any spirits present with the authority of Christ. I will never forget what happened next. The room had darkened with the dusk of late afternoon. Gerhard looked at me with a penetrating gaze and said in his heavy accent, "I hope you know what you're doing." Oh Lord, I thought, I hope *we* know what *we* are doing! I began to pray.

Over the months that followed, I worked with Gerhard, involving others on my prayer team. Finally, a year later, in my office in Corvallis, with five other men present, the Lord graciously broke all remaining bondage and set his servant free. Today, Gerhard and his wife are involved in an outreach ministry to prisoners and street people.

I tell this story to illustrate that in some cases, there is unmistakable oppression that must be dealt with. It is the role of the Spirit of God to expose evil entities that attach to the human personality. Always, in my observation, evil spirits are present for a reason. The bondage traces back to a particular cause, a point of entry, or a lapse in moral life. Why did this deliverance take so long? For one thing, I lacked knowledge. The Lord used this time to toughen me and teach me. Second, the bondage was deep and longstanding—the powers of evil were not willing to let go of this man. This, we found, related to covenants of witchcraft made by Gerhard's ancestors. Third, deeply rooted areas of carnality existed in his life. It took time to identify and bring these areas to the cross. And fourth, this man was of strategic value to the kingdom. There was a real battle for a valuable person. The struggle was long and hard-fought, but in retrospect, the rewards were sweet and the fruit eternal.

It should be clear by now that a right understanding of spiritual warfare requires a broad and holistic view of the human condition, accurate discernment, and wisdom in applying that discernment. Before we explore specific scenarios of oppression, let's take a look at the nature of the enemy we face.

TWO

Understanding Principalities and Powers

People aid his awful designs—the Mafia with its drug and pornography and prostitution businesses, for example. As you can see, so much of what we have around us is inspired by Satan, but he hardly needs to be on call twenty-four hours a day. Advertisers spend billions of dollars to promote so many sinful desires in order to sell their products. . . . Satan created this kind of atmosphere, the moral, spiritual atmosphere which we breathe today. A brilliant chap, this Satan, this Devil, this Lucifer; his handiwork saves him a great deal of legwork.

—Roger Elwood

THE TERM "PRINCIPALITIES AND POWERS" evokes all kinds of mystical mental images. We think of giant, spiritual beings with capes and swords who roam about wreaking havoc on innocent people. Darth Vader of Star Wars fame would certainly come close, a mythical being with a secret source of dark power. Spiritual warfare demands that we gain a working understanding of what these powers really are. My intent here is to make simple an obscure subject. What exactly do we "struggle" against? Who, or what, are these "principalities and powers"?

We know from Ephesians 1:21 and 6:12, and Colossians 1:6 and 2:15, that these are fallen spiritual beings that operate in Satan's domain, opposing the redemptive purposes of God. Often the question arises: where did these evil beings come from? Three separate theories are usually mentioned: they are the disembodied spirits of a pre-Adamic race, destroyed by God (this idea fits with the "gap theory" of creation); they are the "Nephilim" of Genesis 6, the disembodied spirits of a mutant race created by the mating of angels and humans; last, they are of the original angelic creation that fell with Lucifer. I believe the last theory is correct, that we are dealing with fallen angels.

The study of both Old and New Testaments, with additional evidence from Apocryphal texts, reveals three categories of fallen angels: 1. those angels who fell originally with Lucifer at the time of his rebellion and who are still active in the deception and affliction of people; 2. the "sons of God" (angelic beings) of Genesis 6:2 who committed such abominable acts of immorality with the "daughters of men" (women), they were "bound with everlasting chains for judgment on the great Day" (Jude 6); 3. angelic beings who were given charge to watch and rule over certain groupings of mankind. This latter grouping is the least familiar to us. Moses spoke of them:

> When the Most High gave the nations their inheritance, when he divided all mankind, he set up boundaries for the peoples *according to the number of the sons of Israel.* Dt 32:8, emphasis mine

According to the Septuagint text and recent scholarship,

the clearer rendering here is "sons of God," angelic beings (cf. Job 38:7). Daniel 4:13 and 17 call these powers the "Watchers." Who are they? I believe they were angels of a high order endowed with divine authority and appointed to watch over certain segments of humanity. In short, they were spiritual governors. Scripture speaks of the "council of Yahweh," heavenly beings who carry out the divine will (1 Kgs 22:19; Ps 89:6, 7). In light of the Genesis 6 and Jude passages, it seems that it was possible for these powers to lose their positions of authority (Jude 6), and to come under satanic influence (cf. Ps 82:1, 2). Thus, there are powers who seem to have fallen after the fact of Lucifer's rebellion, tempted by their own pride, and usurping positions not ordained by God. D.S. Russell, a scholar of Jewish apocalyptic, captures what may have happened in the spiritual realm:

> There gradually grew up, no doubt under the influence of foreign thought, the notion that the angels to whom God had given authority over the nations and over the physical universe itself, had outstripped their rightful authority and had taken the power into their own hands.... They refused any longer to take their orders from God, but were either rulers in their own right or were prepared to take their orders from someone other than God who, like themselves, had rebelled against the Almighty.[1]

Dualism, however, was foreign to Old Testament theology. The existence of a separate realm of supernatural evil was not clearly perceived. Gradually a post-exilic understanding developed that these powers were separate from God, a source of evil unto themselves. The book of Daniel best reveals this understanding. In my view, these powers coincide with the pagan gods and goddesses worshiped by the Greeks and Romans, territorial deities or "princes" (Dn 10:13, 20) who sought the worship of men. Others became connected with the worship of certain planets and astral bodies (Zeus, Mars, Hermes). Thus, these forces became part of the domain of darkness, manipulated by Satan, the mastermind of deceit.

HELL'S CORPORATE HEADQUARTERS

Paul brings light to the topic by depicting the powers as organized in a hierarchy of rulers/principalities (*archai*), authorities (*exousia*), powers (*dunamis*), and spiritual forces of evil (*kosmokratoras*). It is reasonable to assume the authority structure here is arranged in descending order. Daniel 10:13 and 20 unveil the identity of the *archai* as high level satanic princes set over nations and regions of the earth. The word *exousia* carries a connotation of both supernatural and natural government. In the Apostle's understanding, there were supernatural forces that "stood behind" human structures. Paul no doubt is voicing the Jewish apocalyptic notion of cosmic beings who were given authority by God to arbitrate human affairs. Presumably, the *dunamis* operate within countries and cultures to influence certain aspects of life. The *kosmokratoras* are the many types of evil spirits that commonly afflict people, *e.g.*, spirits of deception, divination, lust, rebellion, fear, and infirmity. These, generally, are the evil powers confronted and cast out in most deliverance sessions. Even among them there is ranking, the weaker spirits subservient to stronger ones.

Until the Judgment, God allows these forces to remain active. The world functions in the tension of a transitional time when victory over darkness has been won, but the redeemed continue to struggle against evil. God allows the adversary to act as tempter and tester. For the individual Christian who submits to God, the schemes of evil serve as tougheners of faith.

These insidious powers continue to work through human governments, religions, and powerful personalities to keep people in bondage to legalism, social ideology, and moral compromise. Their role is to pollute the minds and pervert the wills of people, diverting them from redemption, holding them hostage to the father of lies. When we describe evil at this level, we are in a sense describing the Board Room of Hell, acknowledging that there are high ranking C.E.O.s (Chief Executive Officers) responsible for major movements of deception and destruction in our world. For example, there may be principalities that promote such things as the proliferation of New Age metaphysics, the rise of ritualistic satanism, the production and provision of drugs, the practice of terrorism, sexual perversion, and pornoraphy. There are probably strong, ancient principalities that work through the Hindu caste system of India. Millions are held in bondage to this system of religious legalism.

In 1988, I did some teaching for a missions organization in Colombia. I will never forget the day I arrived at the jungle compound that housed some four hundred Christian workers. By the first evening, I began to notice a crushing weight of oppression closing in around me. I felt unusually vulnerable and threatened. No, it was not just the intense heat and humidity of the jungle climate, nor was it the usual cultural adjustment. As I worked that week, I learned that the compound was surrounded by four major, militant influences: 1. armed Marxist guerrillas fighting to control the country; 2. routes for the transfer of raw coca out of the jungles and into the hands of the cocaine drug lords; 3. tribal Indian groups that practiced witchcraft; 4. militant groups who were vehemently opposed to missionaries.

I also found out that the year before I arrived, a local Colombian had murdered a missionary woman, and had vowed to kill again as soon as he could get out of prison.

By the third or fourth day in this atmosphere, I felt I was being engulfed by an oppressive confusion that made it difficult to function. During the night, I battled as never before with false accusation and discouragement. Was it just my imagination? Was it the stress of a difficult assignment, added to the rigors of life in the jungle? Partially, perhaps. But I have concluded that I and the others at the compound were the targets of spiritual forces opposed to our purpose. Because my task was to instruct the other workers in discernment and spiritual authority, I was a particular target for spiritual attack, the effect of which lingered for weeks after my return home.

Far too many missionary candidates have been sent into such situations untrained in the skills of spiritual warfare, only to return from the field battered and defeated. It is time to take seriously the biblical worldview that depicts front line ministry in terms of armed warfare.

In the spring of 1989 I was privileged to take my family to Israel for ministry and touring. Sitting with the leadership team of a Jewish-Christian congregation in Tel Aviv, I posed the question, "What is it really like being a Jewish believer in this place?" I was ill-prepared for the length and intensity of the response. All of the social, political, and economic discrimination you can imagine was a part of daily life for them. But beyond this, I began to discern the deeper spiritual dynamics that make Christian life in Israel so difficult.

Over the next week, I began to isolate the principalities and powers at work: 1. a militant, spiritual rejection of Jewish Christians by Orthodox groups that is rooted in the rejection of Yeshua as Messiah; 2. a curse of destruction spoken by Muslims committed to the Intifada, the uprising against Israel; 3. a powerful influence of secularism among the non-religious Jews, especially in Tel Aviv; 4. the influx of New Age thought and occultism that seek to fill the need of the Jews for spiritual meaning. The longer we lingered in this land, the more real and intense these influences became to us. Anyone with any sensitivity who walks the streets and corridors of Jerusalem can sense the presence of the Lord and the eternal significance of this city. But one also senses in the atmosphere the conflict of the various spiritual forces that operate behind the religious systems of Judaism, Christianity, and Islam, *and* behind the nationalities and cultures that thrive and strive in Jerusalem.

In any given city, region, country, or group, intelligent spiritual beings work to influence and control the attitudes and behavior of the people. That's the bad news. The good news is that the Holy Spirit is also present in every place, orchestrating the work of the faithful angels intent on revealing truth to men and women whose hearts hunger to know the living God.

MAKING SENSE OF IT ALL

Let me summarize what I believe is an effective approach to spiritual warfare. We began in Chapter One with a multilevel, multifaceted definition that first included conflict between God and Satan, the angels and the demons. So little light is given us on this realm that delving into it is fascinating, but speculative. It makes for stimulating fiction, but it is hard to get a theological handle on it.

The reality of the devil, who holds people hostage to his lies, is more clearly depicted in Scripture. In the parable of the seed and sower (Mt 13:1-23), Jesus interprets the "birds of the air" that steal away the seed as the demons that rob the understanding of truth from one who hears the gospel. Unmistakably, Christians have a role of prayer and authority as they co-labor with the Holy Spirit to break through the demonic blindness that separates men and women from the light of the gospel.

The New Testament describes one role of the Christian as that of soldier, both standing ground and using divine weapons to tear down strongholds of evil. Christians are to *reveal* "to the rulers and authorities in the heavenly realms" the manifold wisdom of God to demonstrate his grace through the cross (Eph 3:10, 11); to *expose* the designs and deeds of darkness (Eph 5:11); to *resist* and stand actively against the devil's schemes (Eph 6:10-18); and to *overcome* the evil one, to conquer his influence over our character (1 Jn 2:12-14).

Most of what you and I deal with daily are the faults, foibles, and physical infirmities of our own natural selves, with all the emotional and psychological baggage that we carry through life. Beyond that, each of us has individual areas of besetting sin that nag at us and drag us down with discouraging regularity. If this were not enough, the covetousness, pleasure, and humanistic appeal of the world system presses upon us all. Now alongside, and sometimes in and through these battles, the devil takes what he can get and aggravates our unresolved emotional problems, besetting sins, and willful blunderings. We are like a finely tuned watch mechanism into which pieces of grit are dropped. What could have functioned well according to original design wears down and malfunctions due to an external, foreign influence.

KEEP YOUR EYE ON THE SPY

In the same sense that a secret agent sends out a signal that merits serious attention by the opposition, so the Christian walking in obedience to the Spirit of God, abiding in prayer, and committed to the kingdom stirs enemy opposition. The stakes are higher for the veteran who can do the most damage to the domain of darkness. My premise should be clear by now: any servant of Jesus Christ who poses a serious threat to the powers of hell will be targeted and will encounter resistance, especially at times of strategic ministry. The anointed agent of Christ's kingdom must be equipped to discern and deal with the efforts of the enemy's kingdom.

A REASSURING WORD

Just because *we* are under attack, doesn't mean we are unprotected. The loving and protective presence of God shields us moment by moment from haphazard assaults. If we sin, the indwelling Spirit immediately goes to work on our conscience to convict us of our transgression. Typically, we squirm for a while. We may rationalize why we did what we did. If this hard-hearted condition persists, we stand in danger of grieving the Spirit. But all the while, he is wooing and working on us to repent and return to him.

If we are following the Spirit and not desiring to make provision for the flesh, we will repent and be forgiven. The "breastplate of righteousness" cleanses our conscience and covers us from the accusative arrows of the enemy. If, however, we persist in our sin, and refuse to deal with it, we may give the devil a "foothold" (Eph 4:27), an opening for his subtle intrusion into our lives. We need to know that God wants us forgiven and shielded from evil more than we do (see Jn. 17:15). Our Lord is greater and more powerful than all the hordes of hell. If our hearts are submitted to him in humility, if we are willing to cleanse our hands of sin and stay committed to his Lordship, then we speak the word "devil, be gone," and it is done (Jas 4:6-10).

Some learning is "caught" in the course of battle, not "taught" in a seminar or learned through a book. Today, we need to be open to allow God to train us to see the subtleties of evil. May God be pleased to raise up men and women equipped to see as he sees, and committed to act with his authority to counteract the kingdom of darkness in our age.

THREE

Preparation for Battle

*Although he is a dark and sinister foe dedicated to the
damnation of humans, I think he knows that it is no
use trying to damn a forgiven and justified child of God
who is in the Lord's hands. So, it becomes the devil's
business to keep the Christian's spirit imprisoned. He
knows that the believing and justified Christian has
been raised up out of the grave of his sins and tres-
passes. From that point on, Satan works that much
harder to keep us bound and gagged, actually
imprisoned in our own grave clothes.*

—A. W. Tozer

THE NEW TESTAMENT TELLS US that Christians continue to face
the enticements and entanglements of evil, and at times
struggle with demonic forces. Paul, Peter, James, and John
all warn us to be on guard against the schemes of the evil
one. The Christian's life is to be characterized by the
praise of God's goodness and glory, not by pessimistic
paranoia. But when evil crosses our path, we are called to
expose, resist, and overcome it. To deny or dodge biblical
warnings is to ignore a central portion of truth.

Various models have been used to describe the operation of supernatural evil in the life of the Christian. Based on the biblical data, I have developed my own approach. Listed below are specific words found in Scripture, and a description of what they appear to mean. Certainly the interpretation is subjective, but it does seem to fit with the clinical reality of counseling encounters.

LEVELS OF EVIL INFLUENCE

LEVEL I: General Warfare Against the Believer

"temptation"	Mt 4:1 Enticement or compulsion: (from an external source) to violate God's law.
SOLUTION:	Resistance (Jas 4:7; 1 Pt 5:9)
"flaming arrows"	Eph 6:16 External influence of evil spirits intended to attack weaknesses or hinder ministry.
SOLUTION:	Armor of God (Eph 6:13-18)

LEVEL II: Specific Bondage, Demonization

"oppression"	Acts 10:38 Persistent, ongoing bondage, affliction of body or soul that may be outward ("vexation") or inward ("demonization").
SOLUTION:	Deliverance (Acts 10:38)

LEVEL III: Deception and Bondage of Unbelievers

"control"   1 Jn 5:19 Dominance of a soul by
                 Satan, either generally (covertly)
                 through deception and dis-
                 obedience (Rv 12:9; Eph 2:2), or
                 specifically (overtly) through the
                 direct control of evil spirits
                 (Mt 8:28-33).

SOLUTION: Salvation (Col 1:13, 14)

To what extent can the believer experience oppression? Clearly, the Christian remains subject to sin and is responsible to forsake it and live free of its power. It is equally clear that the believer remains subject to the influence of the devil and may need deliverance from spirits that afflict either from an outward source or from an inward attachment to an area of the personality. Typically, such spirits gain their influence through pre-conversion sin. They are tenacious, and they must be exposed and expelled. The Christian can thus be "demonized" (Greek: "have a spirit"), but not "possessed." Possession connotes a totality of ownership and control incompatible with the eternal ownership of a soul by God.

Merrill Unger, formerly of Dallas Theological Seminary, and Fred Dickason, currently at Moody Bible Institute, have offered clear biblical justification for this position. Unger's book *What Demons Can Do to Saints* documents his valuable conclusions, both biblical and clinical. But it is Dickason's recent work, *Demon Possession and the Christian,* that offers a sound argument concerning the demonization of believers.

... *daimonizomenos* does not mean owned by a demon, but simply "demonized." This basically describes the condition of a person who is inhabited by a demon or demons and is in various degrees under control with various effects. The idea of ownership is foreign to the New Testament word and its usage. Satan and his demons own nothing. God owns them. They are creatures of God. He is in control of them and determines their limitations and their destiny. They are judged by the cross of Christ, defeated, and bankrupt.[1]

There is a further insight offered by Unger:

It must be stressed that demons cannot indwell a Christian in the same sense that the Holy Spirit indwells. God's Spirit enters a believer at salvation, permanently, never to leave (Jn 14:16). A demon, by contrast, enters as a squatter and an intruder, and is subject to momentary eviction. A demon never rightfully or permanently indwells a saint, as the Holy Spirit does, and no demon can ever have any influence over any part of a Christian's life that is yielded to the Holy Spirit.[2]

I am aware that this position stirs the opposition of many who stand firm with the notion that the Holy Spirit and an evil spirit cannot cohabit the same vessel. But the bottom line is this: Scripture does not exclude the possibility, and clinical reality affirms it time and time again. Personally, I prefer to speak of "influence" rather than cohabitation. Whether a demon buffets me from a mile away, the corner of the room, sitting on my shoulder, whispering in my ear, or clinging to my corruptible flesh, the result is the same.

For those who continue to struggle with whether

demons can oppress Christians, let me offer the following thoughts. First, I appreciate your struggle. At bottom is a spiritual mystery that logic cannot comprehend. I cannot and will not presume to explain how such things can be. But the following considerations have helped me.

First, at conversion, *positional* victory over the devil is secured (Col 2:15) and assured, guaranteed by God (Rom 8:37-39): the Christian is going to heaven. But *practical,* experiential victory over evil must be appropriated and entered into by the exercise of faith (Eph 6:16). We wrongly assume that Satan quits his insidious schemes when someone is converted. The principle also pertains to sin. Positionally, I am justified. Practically, I am responsible to reckon myself dead to sin that still rages in my members, and live a holy life. Does *this* happen automatically, or easily? Most certainly not. Wrestling with the evil one is the same.

A second point is helpful. There is a distinction between the cleansing of the guilt of sin, and dealing with the consequences of sin. One may be forgiven a sinful past, but yet need to face patterns of compulsive behavior, emotional damage, or legal restitution. One may be forgiven something as hideous as the practice of witchcraft, but evil spirits may have staked a claim and may angrily linger in the life of the new Christian, harassing and hindering his or her effectiveness. Satan always seeks to maintain leverage once gained. He does not quit as easily as our neat theologies would like to believe.

There is a third perspective that helps my mind process the problem. Consider that within the personality, there is a distinction between the immaterial essence of the person and the physical body. In fact, Scripture indicates an even finer distinction between the soulish personality (the natural man) and the spirit (the spiritual, or inner man: Heb 4:12 and 1 Thes 5:23). One who is born of the

Spirit may possess salvation, or more correctly, be possessed by God, yet concurrently suffer either bondage to a certain sin, or demonization of the body in a particular area or aspect of the soulish personality. Such a condition offers no threat to salvation.

Paul indicated that the physical body of the Christian is a "temple of the Holy Spirit." Let me offer an analogy to the Old Testament temple. The physical body corresponds to the outer court of the temple, accessible to both Jew and Gentile, a place subject to spiritual contamination. The soul corresponds to the holy place, accessible only to the sanctified Jew. And the spirit of a man is parallel to the holy of holies, accessible only to the priest. Unconfessed sin in the life of the priest brought death in the presence of God. Neither sin nor Satan can occupy the same space filled with the holiness of the Almighty. Within man, there is a separation of the spirit, sanctified and set apart for eternal redemption, from the corruptible aspects of the human soul and body. Thus, a Christian, saved but not yet fully sanctified, may experience bondage to besetting sins or the partial "demonization" of evil spirits.

I realize the conclusion is not comfortable for some, but it does not directly violate scriptural teaching, and it is compatible with clinical realities. Much more could be said about this, but my purpose is not to belabor the point, but to offer practical instruction for those who find themselves struggling with real evil.

DEALING WITH THE DEVIL

Many people mistakenly think that dealing with the evil one requires some deep level of knowledge and a super-spirituality and that it involves a long, laborious struggle. Jesus identified Satan as the "father of lies," the master of deceit. As such, it is the truth of the Word of God that dispels and expels the lies. While many of the devil's devices may appear complex, breaking them is scripturally simple. *Faith* in the supremacy and sufficiency of Jesus' name (Mk 11:22-24; Mt 18:18-20), *confidence* in the power of his atoning blood (Rv 12:11), *courage* to claim and use our authority in resisting evil (Lk 10:19), and total *trust* in the immanent power of the Holy Spirit (Acts 10:38) will break oppression. Dealing with evil requires tools the ordinary Christian has at hand. The Lord will move according to his purpose if conditions for victory are being met. Dealing with the deceiver requires a "go for it" kind of spiritual guts that engages the gears of faith.

Trust the Lord to help you get over hesitation and fear. You will probably feel weak and unprepared. You will sometimes be miserably slow to respond correctly. It always amazes me how so often we know the right way to respond, but fail to do it. You will make mistakes. Don't give up—God will help you. He was there for Moses, Gideon, David, Jeremiah, and others as they stood against evil. He'll be there for you too. To call on his name in a crisis somehow sets in mysterious motion the manifestation of his presence. When you pray and resolve to stand, the Lord of Hosts will show himself strong. Remember, you have the authority to resist evil.

Before we tackle specific forms of oppression in the next two chapters, it would help to learn how to approach warfare. What follows is a streamlined approach that can apply to any type or intensity of spiritual attack.

Pray. First and foremost, anchor your soul in the assurance of the Lord's unfailing presence and love, mindful that nothing in all creation will separate you from him (Rom 8:35ff.). This is a profound promise. *Reaffirm* through praise that God is your source of strength and security. *Repent* of any known sin that would strain your relationship, and then receive forgiveness (1 Jn 1:9). You must be free of Satan's power to accuse (Rv 12:10-11). Remember, holiness removes enemy handles. Ask in prayer for God's wisdom (Jas 1:5, 6) and a sharpening of discernment (1 Jn 2:20, 27). Invite the Holy Spirit to take full control of the circumstance you are facing.

Put on the Armor of God. God's special armor enables the Christian to stand defensively against the devil's wiles. Also, God provides the weapons of his Word and your prayer to repel satanic assaults. The armor should be a regular part of the Christian lifestyle. The challenge is putting on the armor and keeping it on. When you let your guard down, you are vulnerable. Here is a simple reminder of what each piece of armor provides.

Belt of truth: This is the potency of the Word of God, the truth that sets free (Jn 8:31, 32). We must possess a convinced, unshakable conviction in the reliability of Scripture, and a confidence in using the Word of God. We need a decisive determination to trust that what the Lord has spoken will stand.

Breastplate of righteousness: The conscience can be either accused or acquitted. The breastplate is the covering, the cleansing of guilt through the blood of Christ (1 Cor 1:30). To put on this covering is to appropriate on an ongoing basis the Father's forgiveness of our failings and to shield ourselves from false accusation.

Gospel of peace: The soldier's feet are to be "fitted with the readiness that comes from the gospel of peace." Two applications are relevant here. The first is to be ready to reconcile strained or broken relationships (Rom 12:18). Satanic forces work hard to aggravate and exploit divisions within the body of Christ. To restore peace robs the devil of this device. The second application is to be ready to share with the unsaved the message of reconciliation.

Shield of faith: This is in addition to other parts of the armor, and is a general, protective covering. It is an unwavering confidence that what God has promised, he will accomplish (Rom 4:20, 21). The shield has power to "extinguish all the flaming arrows of the evil one." Faith exudes and emits a light that penetrates and eradicates darkness. The man or woman who walks close to God in childlike, trusting faith is a serious threat to the devil.

Helmet of salvation: The child of God can enjoy absolute certainty that he or she belongs to Jesus Christ, eternally. To know and to affirm this is to win the battle of doubt and fear. Satan does not possess the power to snatch a believer from the Father's grip (Rom 8:37-39).

Sword of the Spirit: An offensive weapon, this is the dagger, the *rhema,* the Word of God brought to life through articulation and anointed by the Spirit. Be prepared to speak truth straight out. Jesus used Scripture exclusively to resist and repel Satan (Mt 4:1-11). I have a favorite text, 1 John 3:8: "The reason the Son of God appeared was to destroy the devil's work." A straight, simple, strong jab of the dagger.

Pray in the Spirit: Your prayers, prompted by the Spirit, are guided missiles that penetrate enemy strongholds. We are exhorted to be alert and to pray "for all the saints," *i.e.,* to watch out for and uphold fellow believers in the spiritual battle we all face. Elsewhere we are exhorted to "pray continually" (1 Thes 5:17), walking with an alert sensitivity to the needs around us.

Realize Your Position in Christ. Think of your true identity as enthroned with the Savior (Eph 2:6). In reality you are looking down on the principalities and powers. Meditate on this truth, and let the Lord's authority give you confidence. This is not positive thinking, but the potency of being identified with the risen Lord. Realize that you are resisting in a strength beyond yourself, and that mighty angels, heaven's holy helpers, are assigned to minister to you (Heb 1:14).

Rely on the Supremacy and Sufficiency of Jesus' Name (Phil 2:9-11), on the power of his atoning blood (Col 1:13-20; Rv 12:11). Believe and expect the Spirit of truth to manifest his presence as light that searches out darkness, truth that exposes lies.

Remove the Ground of Oppression. Satanic oppression can be traced to distinct causes. God has established legal parameters, rules that govern this invisible warfare. Moral compromise, deception, and exploitation of vulnerabilities are the chief avenues used to influence people. Doors opened to enemy influence must be shut. Ground given must be reclaimed.

Many pastors, missionaries, counselors, and lay persons have suddenly come face-to-face with a clear case of demonic manifestation. Often they have no formal training in the how-to's of deliverance. But the greatest preparation is pre-occupation with the person of Jesus, and an unshakable faith in his triumph over evil. This fearless faith quickly makes up for any lack of training.

FREE TO FOLLOW

In essence, deliverance from evil provides Christians with an unhindered freedom to follow Jesus. The path of discipleship is hard enough apart from Satan's interference. I want to close this chapter with an encouraging story. It illustrates for us that in many cases dealing with the devil involves a rather simple, straightforward application of truth that has an immediate result.

After teaching a Shabat school class to a Messianic congregation in Tel Aviv, Israel, a young woman came out and told me she had just returned from backsliding and was spiritually oppressed. She looked it. I had no more than five minutes before the start of the worship service, so my assessment needed to be quick. She had been involved with a group that used crystals and pendulums for purposes of divination. "Are you willing to forsake your interest in the occult, return to Yeshua (that's his name there), and submit to him?" I asked. She nodded in immediate agreement. "In the name of Yeshua, I now break the power of any occult spirit attached to this woman and command it to leave." The power of God's Spirit came upon her, and she experienced visible, immediate release. Her confusion cleared up. The tension was gone. We rejoiced in God's goodness and went to worship together. No big deal. No long, drawn-out battle. When the sword of the spirit is used on behalf of one who submits to God, we can expect triumph over the enemy.

FOUR

Common Scenarios of Oppression: The Battle Within

*Who is wise and understanding among you? Let him
show it by his good life, by deeds done in the
humility that comes from wisdom. But if you harbor
bitter envy and selfish ambition in your hearts, do
not boast about it or deny the truth. Such "wisdom"
does not come down from heaven but is earthly,
unspiritual, of the devil. For where you have envy
and selfish ambition, there you find disorder and
every evil practice.* Jas 3:13-16

"HOW RELEVANT IS DEMONIC ACTIVITY to the daily life of the
average Christian? Isn't there a danger of inventing
bogeymen who aren't really there?"

These were questions raised by an alert housewife
tenaciously pressing me to prove that training in discernment and spiritual authority were necessary items in
the arsenal of today's believer.

The Holy Spirit can help us to discern the lines between the physical, psychological, social, and spiritual dimensions of daily life. Hebrews 4:12, 13 says: "For the Word of God is living and active, sharper than any two-edged sword, piercing to the division of soul and spirit . . . and discerning the thoughts and intentions of the heart. And before him no creature is hidden, but all are open and laid bare to the eyes of him with whom we have to do."

This chapter and the next present five examples of spiritual oppression and explain how to deal with it. Satan can attack us in our minds and emotions (internally) or in our situations, relationships, and circumstances (externally). The two primary weapons he uses against us internally are the *undermining of our conscience* and *sin-based oppression*. These are the focus of this chapter. The three main arenas of external attack are discussed in the next chapter.

SCENARIO 1: EROSION OF CONSCIENCE

Back in the early 1980s, residents living in the Love Canal area of western New York State started to exhibit an unusually high frequency of cancer and leukemia. A search led to the discovery of toxic wastes that had leaked into residential water tables, infecting hundreds of families. These unsuspecting people were living right on top of life-threatening chemicals, but were unaware that these unseen toxins were slowly seeping into their bodies. In a similar way, individualism, secularism, and relativistic values have created an environment that envelops us and conditions our way of thinking. Those of us who live in affluent societies know that we are facing a battle for the preservation of biblical values.

Increased exposure to immorality and vulgarity leads

to a diminished ability to discern good from evil. In the January 1989 issue of *Citizen,* a magazine produced by Focus on the Family, John Evans, head of Movie Morality Ministries states:

> With this degeneracy in movies, one would expect that most Christians would be greatly offended by it and refuse to go. Tragically, this is not the case. Christians have been seduced into accepting degenerative movie content, and many have simply lost a sensitivity to vulgarity, sexual explicitness, brutal violence, and ungodly lifestyles in the movies.

In an indirect sense, compromises like this give room for the devil.

Dealing with a Compromised Conscience. 1. *Realize,* with transparent honesty, which values of pagan culture you have embraced or tolerated, *e.g.,* covetousness, ambition, lust, intellectual pride, to name a few. Admit compromises to the Lord and to at least one trusted Christian friend.

2. *Repent* of lines crossed in your conscience. Allowing yourself to be exposed to sensuality, to indulge in materialism, or to seek worldly prestige are typical traps. Boldly ask Jesus to put this area of your life on the cross and to render it powerless (see Gal 5:24, 25).

3. *Regain* the perspective of holiness, and recommit your heart to hunger first of all for a pleasing relationship with the Lord. Return to sections of Scripture that describe godly values, *e.g.,* Proverbs, the Sermon on the Mount, 1 Timothy, 1 Thessalonians. Read a biography of one of the great saints who led a holy life. Your heart will follow after what your mind chooses to dwell on.

4. *Reaffirm* kingdom values of servanthood, generosity, hospitality, honesty, and so on. Record your decisions in

the margin of your Bible or in a journal. Set your course, individually, as a couple, or as a family to pursue holiness as a citizen of the kingdom of heaven.

SCENARIO 2: SIN-BASED OPPRESSION

Unresolved sin gives Satan a foothold, a "legal" ground on which he can stand and a position from which he can oppress you. Not every moral compromise results in oppression, though. For many, receiving forgiveness from God is all the protection necessary. It remains somewhat a mystery to me why one person ends up oppressed and another does not. Nevertheless, oppression is very often the result of personal sin. There are three areas of sin that can leave Christians vulnerable to oppression: pre-conversion, generational, and post-conversion.

PRE-CONVERSION SIN

When leading people to Christ, we can do them a great service by encouraging thorough repentance and renunciation of sin that will separate them from the habits of their past and break the influence of evil spirits. Such bridge-burning exercises should be a normal part of personal evangelism. It is important to have people verbally claim Christ's ownership of them and to command any evil spirits present to leave them permanently, and to forbid them to return. It also helps to explain to a new convert the need for taking a personal stand of faith and resistance against evil.

Colossians 1:13, 14 is clear: "For he has rescued us from the dominion of darkness and brought us into the kingdom of the Son he loves, in whom we have redemption, the forgiveness of sins." The believer's "membership records" are transferred from one kingdom to another, and the devil's main work of diverting his soul from eternal salvation is thwarted. But another insidious goal is still relevant: to hinder the growth and fruitfulness of the child of God. It is wrong to assume that the devil loses interest and gives up the fight.

If the enemy has established a foothold based in the sins of your former life, he may yet try to work it to his advantage. As a believer you are forgiven, justified, and destined for heaven, but if Satan's footholds are not dealt with, you remain a target for oppression.

I once held a meeting at a church in Oregon's Willamette Valley. After the Friday night service, a burly, bearded man came up to me and shot my lecture full of holes: "I can't buy this business that a Christian can have demons!" I told him he was entitled to his opinion. The next morning I started into a day of counseling. He was the first to show up, conceding to pressure from his wife. Things were not well at home. He explained that he had a ministry of worship, but every time he got involved in church, "all hell broke loose." He got depressed, his anger flared, and he felt like leaving the faith. "I don't believe in what you're doing," he told me, "but go ahead, there might be something to this." He put his arms in the air, and with a desperate resignation exclaimed, "Do me, man!" So, I "did him."

I proceeded with a brief interview and learned that prior to conversion, he had experimented heavily with hallucinogenic drugs and had friends who practiced spiritualism. Truthfully, I didn't expect any demonic activity. In many cases, spirits are driven away at conversion. Pressed for time, I went directly into prayer: "In the authority of Jesus Christ, I command to attention any enemies of Christ assigned to Rick to ruin his marriage and hinder his ministry. I call into the light any spirits that came to him through indulgence with drugs." That's as far as I got. Rick was already experiencing an unmistakable manifestation of an evil presence, causing dizziness, visual hallucination, and nausea. As he struggled to understand what was happening to him and to justify it theologically, I asked him if he was willing to forsake all sin, past and present, and receive fresh forgiveness from the Lord. He readily agreed, and we prayed. Then, with a simple command, the tension lifted, and the presence was gone. Together we rejoiced in the power of Jesus' name.

This illustration is typical of a pre-conversion "foothold" that was never fully broken. These spirits, having once gained influence, hang on and count on their ability to entrap their victim in the same sin again. Other pre-conversion sins which give Satan a foothold for oppression are: forms of occultism like playing with ouija boards, seeking out fortune tellers or other forms of divination, and going to seances. I have also found that evil spirits sometimes attach to those who are victims of incest or violent sexual crime. Unresolved bitterness and hatred toward another person may also invite lingering oppression.

Dealing with Pre-Conversion Sin. The clearest instruction about dealing with our sin is found in James 4:4-10. I want simply to list some steps involved in finding spiritual freedom. You can pray this on your own if you suspect you are oppressed; however, I advise you to ask for the aid of a fellow Christian familiar with spiritual warfare. Understand that this passage applies to dealing with any form of oppression, not merely the kind that lingers from the sins of the pre-conversion life. If no evil spirits are involved, there will be no manifestation, only a quiet process of confession and cleansing.

1. *Be willing to separate your life from the world, and to be a friend only to God.* Our Lord jealously desires each of us to abide in a love relationship with him. Attachment to

idols—money, ambition, pride, may leave one an enemy of God, and a target of the arch-enemy. Our Father longs for the loyalty of our love.

2. *Submit to God in brokenness and humility.* Make an earnest effort to forsake all pride and to come near to him. He waits to be wanted. Grace is freely given to the one whose spirit is broken and contrite.

3. *Wash your hands of any known sin.* Repent, and receive the washing of forgiveness that puts the devil to flight. A clear conscience is a key to victory in warfare. All rationalizations and justifications have to be nailed to the cross. Verbally confess anything that separates you from fellowship with the Father.

4. *Purify your heart from any doubleminded wavering.* The Lord is a jealous Master. He wants to know he is your first love. He commands our commitment. Fencesitters are fair and foolish game for the devil. Doubt, mistrust, and duplicity must be forsaken.

5. *Realize how serious your struggle with the world, the flesh, and the devil really is.* Flippant, half-hearted attitudes are inappropriate when seeking the presence of the Lord.

6. *Resist the devil.* There is no substitute for taking personal responsibility to act in the authority of Christ's name, commanding the devil to flee. If the prior conditions are met, all enemies of Christ must and will go.

If you are under sin-based oppression, seek and submit to God, repent of sin and doublemindedness, and grieve over your condition. When you make the additional choice of resisting the devil, God will fulfill two promises: he will draw near to his struggling child, and he will drive the devil off.

Having carefully worked through this passage from James, I often lead an oppressed person through the following prayer. Understand this is not a formula, but a pattern of how to take ground from the enemy and regain grace from above.

Prayer for Removing Oppression

Lord, I call to you in the name of Jesus, my High Priest. I submit to your will. I invite your Spirit to search and convict me of any sin (confess any current sin before continuing). Thank you for your forgiveness and cleansing—I put on your breastplate of righteousness. I ask you, on my behalf, to expose all schemes of Satan ever devised against me, through any source, at any time. I ask you, Holy Spirit, to bring into the light powers of darkness that may oppress me.

I forsake all sin in my blood ancestry that may have opened doors to darkness _____ (specify names of relatives and sins, if relevant). I close these doors as they relate to me and my children _____ (name your children). I forsake all personal sin that has given ground to the enemy. I reclaim that ground now. Lord Jesus, I apply the power of your name and blood to remove from me all consequences of evil oppression. In your authority, I break the binding effect of all curses (be specific, if possible, *e.g.,* witchcraft, hatred, etc.), spells, charms, hexes, vexes, psychic powers, works of witchcraft . . . anything of evil ever put upon me from any source. I ask you, Lord Jesus, to bind together all enemy spirits that may oppress me, and remove them from my life. Deliver me from all evil.

Spoken with sincerity and authority, this prayer will be effective in loosing the grip of satanic forces present. If you are praying on behalf of another person, you may also give direct command to the enemy to take flight:

Command of Resistance

I expose all enemies of Jesus Christ operative against _____ . I sever you from Satan and any power above you. I remove your right to afflict _____, and proclaim your judgment under the hand of God. I weaken you with the blood of Calvary. In the authority of Christ, I bind all spirits present together. I command you to go where Jesus Christ tells you to go, by the voice of his Spirit, and by the voice of his servant now speaking.

Many variables operate in deliverance: the condition of the heart, the strategic value of a person to the kingdom, family strongholds that have persisted through generations, the lack of knowledge and faith of the person in charge, to name just a few. Some spirits only come out through the sacrifice of prayer and fasting. Often God allows us to learn lessons in the process. Keep close to him. Listen and learn what he wants to teach. If this process results in release and resolution, thank God and go on. If after it you do not feel clear or clean, then seek further help from a discerning fellow believer.

GENERATIONAL SIN

Those who have had experience with deliverance know that in some cases there are demonic powers that have worked within a family bloodline for many generations. This phenomenon is clinically documented.

A principle of divine judgment that inspires both fascination and fear is found in Exodus 20, in the record of the revelation of the Ten Commandments. After forbidding the practice of idolatry, the Lord speaks:

You shall not bow down to them or worship them; for I, the LORD your God, am a jealous God, *punishing the children for the sin of the fathers to the third and fourth generation of those who hate me,* but showing love to thousands who love me and keep my commandments.

Ex 20:5, 6, emphasis mine

The same idea is repeated in Exodus 34:7, and a similar expression is used by the prophets, particularly in Jeremiah 32:18: "You show love to thousands but bring the punishment for the fathers' sins into the laps of their children after them." Obviously, there is a stiff penalty for idolatry and rebellion, for spurning the love and favor of Yahweh. We see, by observing the sons of the priest Eli, and the trouble David had with his sons, that the consequence of a father's sin falls into the lap of future generations. The spiritual law of sowing and reaping plays itself out through the principle of solidarity with or connectedness to ancestors. In short, my true identity is not merely "Tom White" but "John Gordon White's son." What happens to this principle under the new covenant? Is it superseded by salvation through grace, obtained by simple, individual faith?

Anyone who works long enough with people will notice that certain family behaviors, both desirable and undesirable, are repetitive. Thus, a father who models discipline and faithfulness may inculcate these traits in his son. On the other hand, a man who is given to lust and indulgence in pornography, or a man who cannot control his temper, may pass on these weaknesses to his children. Such traits vary from physical indulgences, to attitudes of criticism and bitterness, to anger. Are these only learned behaviors? What if distinct traits of a grandfather show up in a grandson even though the two have had very little contact? Are these transmitted genetically? Perhaps. Very likely both genetic predisposition *and* learned behavior interact with each other.

But I must mention a third possibility: the activity of "familial" spirits that operate in connection with family lineage. The devil attacks and exploits unconfessed sin. If sin occurs, especially sin related to idolatry or witchcraft, and it remains unresolved, the enemy has a legal right to accuse and oppress. Combining the biblical principle of the visitation of the sins of the fathers on the children with clinical data from deliverance sessions, we observe a connection between genealogical sin and oppression in current generations. Satan's goal is to perpetuate his strongholds.

Let me relate a hypothetical illustration. Let's say that my great-grandmother practiced occultism. She would have consorted with spirits and received certain powers of divination. She went to her grave unrepentant and unredeemed, her sin unresolved before God. What happens to those divining and deceiving spirits when she dies? Where do they go? They will probably try to stay within the family. The typical scenario is that these spirits will transfer to the daughter, or granddaughter, or jump over to the male line. The spirits claim a right to remain in the family based on the unrepentant or unresolved sin. A generation or two later, I enter the picture and find my way into the kingdom of God. If, at the time of conversion, I do not sufficiently separate and break from these spiritual connections, I may experience some significant oppression arïd resistance to my growth in grace.

Several summers back I was asked to teach at a missionary organization. I finished my lecture, and was approached by a young man who looked troubled. He asked for time to talk. I fumbled around for my appointment book, only to hear Rob's insistence, "*Now*, I have to talk to you *now*." We moved into a more suitable room, and we began to talk. The heaviness and darkness surrounding him was palpable. As I asked him questions about his life, he looked increasingly anxious and uttered the very same words Gerhard had: "I hope you know what you're doing. There's something here that wants to tear you apart."

Rob explained that to his knowledge, he was the only believer in his family. He had wanted to be a missionary since his teen years. Now on the field, he experienced regular depression, suicidal impulses, and violent temper. His marriage was strained, and he was about to give up. He told me about his grandfather, who had run alcohol illegally into the United States from Canada in the 1920s and who was reputed to have been a murderer. Once I had enough data, I pressed ahead in prayer. I commanded any spirits present connected to Rob's grandfather to come to immediate attention and to present themselves by direct impression on Rob's mind.

There was an observable surge of violent anger that surfaced. He reported back to me, "Something is here—whatever it is hates you and is threatening your life. There is a voice inside me saying, 'back off from this, or we will get your family.'" I pressed on and demanded that the ruling spirit make itself clearly known by impression through Rob's mind. Immediately, Rob experienced spiritual insight into the identity of the spirit, a separate, internal voice reacted to my exercise of authority, boasting of its violent nature, and its plans for the destruction of Rob's marriage and ministry. Without question, this was an alien, cunning spirit distinct from his personality. It admitted that it had come from the grandfather and had been transferred to Rob shortly after his death. The struggle that followed was not easy. Rob went through some physical discomforts, and I was relying on the strength of the Holy Spirit to provide me with extra stamina. Two hours later, the enemy admitted defeat and departed with an angry, convulsive shudder. The weight of an ancestral curse had been lifted from one of God's servants. To this day, Rob and his wife are pursuing fruitful ministry, facing the trials of life common to all Christian workers, but free of the intense oppression.

Let me strongly caution you at this point. Do not dash to your drawer, search for a copy of your family tree, and begin to investigate your background. If this teaching has bearing on your own life, the Holy Spirit will speak and prompt you to consider it. If after prayer, reflection, and counsel with another mature Christian, these illustrations seem to fit your situation, you may proceed with the process that follows and effectively separate yourself from the sin and satanic oppression of former generations.

Dealing with Generational Sin. 1. *Recognize sources, or entry points, of possible oppression.* If you suspect a stronghold, search out names of relatives and the type of sin or bondage that may have opened a door to demonic infiltration.

2. *Pray according to the instruction of Leviticus 26:40, 42.* Confess your own sins, and those of your fathers, especially sins related to rebellion against God and hatred of others. When the Israelites did this in a spirit of humility, God said he would remember his covenant with Jacob and remember the land. In short, there will be a restoration of divine favor.

3. *Deliberately forgive those in your ancestry who sinned.* Don't fall into the trap of carrying bitterness against anyone. Give up the grudges and bring resolution to strained relationships.

4. *Partake of the Lord's supper.* There is power released in the observance of communion. Encouraging the church at Corinth to separate itself from pagan idolatry, Paul states in 1 Corinthians 10:16-21 that ". . . you cannot partake of the table of the Lord and the table of demons." This should be a time of reaffirmation of your commitment to the Lord and a formal removal of ground claimed by Satan.

5. *Pray with authority in Jesus' name* to separate your life (and your children's lives) from the sins of former generations. This is like building a dam, cutting off the

flow of evil influence. Here is an example of how you might pray:

> Heavenly Father, I confess the wickedness of my earthly father, his sexual sin and violent anger. I forsake and separate myself and my children from those sins. God, be gracious to me. In Jesus' authority, I now apply the power of his blood to break all curses and consequences of evil that may have entered my family.

After this prayer, it is wise to utter a verbal command to rid your life of any familial spirits. Tell the enemy he has no legal claim to continue working in your family.

The Old Covenant principle of Leviticus 26 is very clear. While some would question whether such an effort is necessary in light of the grace of the New Covenant, this procedure has helped bring relief from the oppression of spiritual bondage rooted in the past.

POST-CONVERSION SIN

Leviticus 11:44, 45 records the words of the Lord: "be holy, because I am holy." This injunction is repeated in 1 Peter 1:15. The Lord wants our character to be like his own. Under the New Covenant, he gave us the indwelling of the Holy Spirit, who gives us power to walk in holiness. John tells us that if we claim to be without sin, we are self-deceived. But if we honestly acknowledge sin, God will graciously cleanse our unrighteousness (1 Jn 1:8, 9).

God chose Israel to receive his favor and unconditional love. He promised his blessing if they would love and obey him in return. When rebellion occurred, God used foreign oppressors to discipline his people. They remained under domination and captivity until they were broken and purged. In similar fashion, the Lord today gives over the persistent backslider to the oppressive power of Satan, for the primary purpose of correction. The Corinthian man caught in sexual sin was turned over to Satan for the "destruction of his flesh" (1 Cor 5:4, 5). Hymenaeus and Alexander were two backsliders whom Paul turned over to Satan, "to be taught not to blaspheme" (1 Tm 1:20). The point is this: when a sinning Christian ignores or resists the Holy Spirit's conviction and does not confess, there is a very real danger of temporarily coming under the adversary's power.

Dealing with Post-Conversion Sin. After a teaching session in a local church, a woman phoned to make an appointment. On a hot July day I listened to Eva's confession of indulging in sex and drugs. In addition, she had become obsessed with videos loaded with explicit sex, violence, and occultism. She had come to salvation years earlier but had slipped back into sin. Based on my warning that unresolved sin can invite bondage, she opened her life anew to the Lord. Moments after her prayer, she began to experience troubling physical symptoms: she could not focus her eyes, her limbs began to shake, and her breathing was difficult. We had to pray many times for nearly a year to get rid of spirits of fear, lust, destruction, and witchcraft.

What began to amaze me, and greatly trouble Eva, was that God seemed to be in no real hurry to free her from these evil forces. I assigned her Bible passages to meditate on and books to read on deliverance and holy living. We worked through some areas of struggle in her life and weakened the grip of the demons through continued authoritative prayer. Eva began to treasure her relationship with God and to grow in grace. One day the Spirit prompted me to pursue Eva's final deliverance. His power was present, and she was finally free. But through the process, Eva told me to pass on this message to as many fellow Christians as possible: "Sin is serious business—don't let the devil get a handle on your life!" Eva now works in a Christian foster home for delinquent girls, bearing fruit for the Lord and warning of the dangers of sin to anyone who will listen.

God is more desirous that we succeed in our walk of holiness than we are. When we sin, the Shepherd of our souls reaches out his crook first to gently touch us, letting us know we are out of line and inviting us to return to him. If we resist his overtures, he can allow us to experience the pressure and pain of either natural consequences or supernatural oppression.

FIVE

Common Scenarios of Oppression: The Battle from Without

We are hard pressed on every side, but not crushed;
perplexed, but not in despair; persecuted but not
abandoned; struck down, but not destroyed.

2 Cor 4:8, 9

IF THE DEVIL HAS NO LEGAL BASIS on which to accuse and afflict us, he resorts to methods of buffeting us by external harassment. When Paul says that we contend with the "flaming arrows of the evil one," he describes the attack against our minds, wills, and emotions. This commonly takes the form of excessive or unfounded irritation, bitterness, criticism, lustful impulses, jealousy, and fear. There are enemy spirits with such names and functions who try to exploit or distort our natural emotional responses to life's vicissitudes. Scenario 3 outlines this type of external attack.

Have you ever come away from a particular person or a specific place with the feeling that you had just been in contact with something "not quite right"? Maybe it felt like a fog bank suddenly rolled in and left you confused, weak in faith, and fearful. Maybe you just felt an indefinable sense of the presence of darkness. The simple premise here is that certain persons and places are "carriers" of a demon's presence. I discuss this form of external attack in Scenario 4.

Finally, anyone who is called to serve in Christian leadership will, to some degree, face the type of trials that test character and faith that I cover in Scenario 5. In fact, as Paul wrote in 2 Timothy 3:12, "Everyone who wants to live a godly life in Christ Jesus will be persecuted."

These three scenarios are typical forms of external abuse and attack which Satan uses to harass us and to undermine our confidence. Each of these situations, however, can be dealt with in the authority of Christ. The Lord has graciously provided us with spiritual armor for defense, spiritual weapons for offense, and the Holy Spirit to guide us as we grow in wisdom and discernment.

SCENARIO 3: FLAMING ARROWS

Have you ever had thoughts leap into your mind that seemed completely out of character, bizarre, and shocking? Thoughts of leaving your mate and children, thoughts of doing something violent to get even with someone who hurt you, plans to indulge in sinful behavior? In the confidentiality of the counseling relationship, I have heard many such inner impressions revealed. People desperately want to know: is this thought normal? Am I sick, or crazy? Sometimes there are psychiatric disorders that contribute to such thought patterns. But in many cases, these conscious fantasies and unconscious dreams emanate from the weakness of our own character or the temptation to sin. And these weaknesses toward violence or indulgence may be exploited and stirred up by the invisible enemies that surround us.

What's going on here? Without adopting an automatic "blame-it-on-the-devil" attitude in the hopes of shirking our own responsibility, we need to remember that we *do* live in an unseen spiritual world inhabited by intelligent beings who promote good and evil. To what extent do they interact with our daily lives? I am convinced that the weaknesses in our nature and in our characters can be triggered by certain tensions in our relationships or in our environment. Evil spirits can then exploit those vulnerable moments. When we do not yield to the control of the Holy Spirit, we become potential targets for evil spirits to provoke the intensity of attitudes and actions that originate in the sin nature itself.

In Ephesians 6, Paul uses the imagery of battle to describe spiritual warfare. The "flaming arrows" refer to arrows which had been dipped in a flammable pitch designed to set clothing or roofs ablaze. Spiritual "flaming arrows" may take such forms as lust, fear, doubt rage, thoughts of suicide, fear of insanity, accusation, and hatred. They emanate from an external source and stick to a vulnerable area of a person's mind, will, emotions, or even body, especially when the shield of abiding faith drops down. So many times I have heard it said: "something came over me," or, "something hit me, and I blew up—I could have killed someone!" The purpose of the flaming arrow is to tempt or compel a vulnerable Christian into committing sin.

James seems to make the best summation of human carnality. He states that a person is tempted "when, by his own evil desire, he is dragged away and enticed" (1:14). The desire, the thought, when acted upon, gives birth to sin, the act. There is a constant, day in and day out battlefield in the mind. How do you know the difference between an evil desire lurking in the mind, as distinct from a "flaming arrow"? Frankly, it is hard to answer that question. Is this impulse to anger coming from my own weak character, or is it the devil's doing? Let's probe this a bit. My own evil desire will probably be all too familiar to me, a predictable pattern I've battled with. The Holy Spirit is also quick to convict me of my own sinfulness. Flaming arrows, on the other hand, come like a shot out of the blue, with a nearly irresistible intensity. With such assaults there is also often confusion and excessive guilt, especially if it was an angry impulse which unleashed its fury on another person.

Dealing with Flaming Arrows. When negative thoughts shoot into the mind like spears, the best response is to follow Jesus' example of speaking truth. Three times he addressed Satan with the words, "It is written," then concluded the encounter with the rebuke, "Away from me, Satan! For it is written, 'Worship the Lord your God, and serve him only'" (Mt 4:10). At times it is crucial to identify the lie and tell the devil to take an immediate hike. But let's also understand that there are strongholds of the mind that must be brought under the control of the Spirit. Whether an impression originates from within or without, we have a choice. Paul says that "*We* demolish arguments and every pretension that sets itself up against the knowledge of God, and *we* take captive every thought to make it obedient to Christ" (2 Cor 10:5). We have a responsibility either to cut off our thoughts before they give birth to sin, or to rebuke the whisperings of the enemy. Though most of us know this, many of us are not decisive enough about responding.

By reaffirming your confidence in God, the shield of faith acts as a fire retardant that quenches the flaming arrows. The Roman shield was a two-and-a-half by four-foot rectangle that protected vital parts of the body. All a man had to do was hold on to the shield, and point it in the right direction! Affirm God's faithfulness. Cling to him as a rock. Take refuge in his name. Remind yourself, and the devil, *whose* you are.

SCENARIO 4: ATTACK THROUGH A PERSON OR PLACE

Terri and I have some very close friends on the mission field who have had considerable exposure to spiritual warfare. Whenever they return from furlough to their assignment with an Indian tribal group in Canada, they describe the place on the highway where they cross into the "territory." Numerous times now they have documented a tangible oppression that affects their minds, mood, and physical energy level. What is happening here? Most likely fallen spirits are at work in the environment. They are connected to certain places or people and their activity may be perceived by those gifted with discernment.

A few years ago, I was experiencing weariness and stress in my ministry. My shield of faith was getting badly dented. A friend offered us his home on the coast, so we took a much-needed family retreat.

Late in the afternoon one day at low tide, we were poking about looking for shells and starfish. We had wandered under a restaurant perched on large wooden posts. My wife Terri and I have developed a sensitivity to spiritually dark places. We both sensed something threatening about this area. We signaled to the kids and headed up the embankment. Later that night, after getting the children to bed, Terri and I agreed that in the vicinity of the restaurant, we had both felt fearful.

Retiring at about 11:30, I made an effort to go to sleep. But I was being assaulted with a barrage of uncontrollable fear. I was besieged with the vivid but seemingly un-reasonable thought of drug-crazed hitchhikers smashing through the windows and attacking my family. Eventu-ally Terri and I jumped out of bed and got onto our knees to pray through the spiritual storm raging about us. The terror subsided, and we fell asleep.

After returning home, I related the experience to some friends. They informed me that the seaside restaurant onto whose grounds we had wandered was a gathering place for drug sellers and biker gangs from up and down the coastline.

Have you ever come away from contact with a place, such as a New Age bookstore, a movie theater, or a restaurant and found yourself feeling fearful or confused? When this happens, don't be so quick to ignore your feelings or rationalize them. Ask the Holy Spirit for discernment. Be quick to respond with prayer for pro-tection. As ambassadors of an invisible kingdom, we simply need to understand the reality behind the veil of visible events. We may unknowingly find ourselves caught between the clashing of kingdoms, light and dark, truth and falsehood.

Dealing with Direct Assaults. 1. *Trace the presumed spiritual attack directly to the source.* Spiritual oppression does not occur on a coincidental or haphazard basis. Ask the question, "When did I start feeling this way?" Are the symptoms associated with your contact with a specific person or locality? This discernment is a major part of resolving the problem. It is gained primarily by following the promptings of the Holy Spirit, and you may need to seek the help of others better gifted with discernment and spiritual authority.

2. *Face the attack head-on.* When faced with these things, our human tendency is to avoid direct confrontation.

Emissaries of the evil one do their most effective work through lies, bluffs, and threats. A believer who is backed into a corner of doubt and fear will be buffeted. If, however, there has been no moral compromise that allows for valid accusation, the right response is to stand up to the devil and speak the Scripture, as Jesus did: " 'The reason the Son of God appeared was to destroy the devil's work' (1 Jn 3:8). Satan, leave me now." Much of the unnecessary oppression in our lives is caused either by naivete or ignorance, a lack of training in the skills of spiritual warfare.

3. *Erase the effects of the assault.* If the harassment of the enemy is not ordained by God for a clear purpose, then act immediately to shake off its lingering effects. I suggest a prayer similar to the following. Please note, there is a clear distinction between prayer (communion with the Lord) and resistance using the authority of Jesus to personally resist the evil one:

Prayer

Heavenly Father, I call to you in the strength and authority of Jesus. I am your servant, and I submit to your will. Lord, in the power of your name, and through the power of Jesus' blood, I ask you to shield me with your presence and deliver me from this evil. I stand against any forces of evil that have brought this oppression and break their power over my mind and emotions. Holy Spirit, give light to my mind, liberty to my spirit, and anoint my words with your power.

Resistance

In the authority of Jesus Christ, I command any enemies of Christ sent to or assigned to me to leave now, never to return. I expose you and place you under the judgment of God Most High. I conquer you with the blood of Christ.

4. *Break the power of any curses you sense may have been placed on you.* (See the appropriate prayer in Chapter Ten.) Be careful not to repay evil with evil. After breaking the curse or spell with the blood of Christ, verbally bless the perpetrator and pray for his or her salvation. Paul reaffirmed Jesus' teaching: "When we are cursed, we bless" (1 Cor 4:12).

SCENARIO 5: CATCHING FLAK ON THE CUTTING EDGE

Paul knew the misunderstanding of men, the harassment of political and religious leaders, and the spiritual oppression of demonic powers. He begins and ends 2 Corinthians 4 with an affirmation, "we do not lose heart." To identify with the Lord Jesus is to enter into his suffering.

Though the Apostle does not specifically mention demons, the reality of spiritual warfare is made obvious by his words. He refers often to the pain of misunderstanding and rejection from both believers and non-believers. Certainly he must also have thought of the many circumstances when evil men wanted him killed. The devil used whomever or whatever he could to dissuade Paul from his commission. Paul's example teaches me that pain is at one and the same time both purposeful and deeply paradoxical. I am comforted to know that my troubles are producing an eternal glory that will one day supersede the worst misery endured on earth. But on an immediate, emotional level, hardship can produce a weight that crushes my confidence. It is easy to wonder why the Israelites were so rebellious when they had the Red Sea experience, the pillar of fire at night, and the cloud of God's presence by day. Yet we are made of the same stuff and fall prey to the same sins.

We have a profoundly important decision to make in the midst of trial: we can break *down,* and give in to doubts about God's promise or purpose in pain, or we can hold steady and break *through* to a deeper level of character. Sooner or later most Christians go through a time of testing when they are tempted to shout to the heavens, "Where is the victory here?" Certainly this is evident in the Bible, which portrays many of God's people groping to understand why the righteous have such trouble. Each one had to wrestle with the issue and to decide that God was to be trusted. True spiritual victory emerges from the crucible of suffering. A Christian's capacity to overcome the world, the flesh, and the devil must be tested, and sometimes to the limit.

Perhaps you have labored through seasons of prolonged confusion and discouragement, when the well of God's presence seems to have dried up. St. John of the Cross called this the "dark night of the soul." No doubt you have known the acute pain of being unjustly criticized or betrayed. Others know the misery of grappling with an emotional or psychological thorn of weakness that seems to take God forever to touch and heal. In relationship to spiritual warfare, here is the point: the devil seems to work overtime to misdirect the mind and manipulate the emotions of suffering Christians, who are tempted to cry out, "God, this is not fair. You are not fair. If this is the abundant Christian life, I don't want it!"

Who wants his character refined by the fire of testing? No one. If our character development plan were left to us, most of us would avoid such testings and end up spiritual flyweights. And so we derive comfort by pondering the deep truths of Hebrews 12, which shows God as our loving Father shaping and molding us, through discipline, into perfection. One of the things that will help us in the process is to distinguish the whisperings of the father of lies from the loving voice of our heavenly Father.

Dealing with Trial. 1. *Ask the Lord if this suffering is purposeful.* When Paul sought the Lord for the removal of his thorn (2 Cor 12), God gave him peace and grace to accept the thorn as something productive of humility. If God gives you a similar answer, ask him, in light of Hebrews 12, "What am I to learn here? How can I grow, not in spite of, but in light of this trial?" If, on the other hand, you are enduring unnecessary enemy harassment, you have the authority to rebuke it through direct command. Seek the counsel and discernment of others close to you, who may be able to see God's purposes more clearly.

2. *Make a choice to turn your self-pity into triumph.* If somehow I can choose to thank God for the trial, and praise him for his purposes, he will pour out grace to grow. You may need to get quite practical here and decide to take specific steps to restore a strained relationship or seek out counseling for a longstanding emotional weakness that *can* and *should* be healed.

3. *Anchor your soul in God's unfailing attributes.* Review the Scriptures that reveal the character of the Lord, and affirm his goodness, through prayer and praise, his unfailing love, his quickness to forgive and restore a floundering child.

4. *Rebuke the father of lies.* Let the devil and his minions know that you are choosing to trust the goodness of God, no matter what.

Jesus, anticipating the agony of Gethsemane, made a significant statement to his disciples: "The prince of this world is coming. He has no hold on me" (Jn 14:30). He was fully free of any rights the enemy hoped to have over him. He was strong in the security of sonship. The same can be true for you and me. Though spiritual warfare will be of concern to the close of the age, we can come to say with Jesus, "He has no hold on me." This will never mean freedom from external trial and tribulation. What I am talking about is a freedom *of* the spirit, a confidence and a courage that conquers the worst devices of the devil.

A mark of maturity is to rejoice in tribulation. Spiritual warfare is a great opportunity to exemplify the character of our Lord. When I walk in grace, the Father says, "Look, there, that's my son!" The devil is defeated in the face of a son who takes his Father at his word and walks by faith, no matter how tough the trials get. To incarnate the obedient submission of Jesus is to destroy the will and works of Satan and to demonstrate the goodness and glory of God.

SIX

Am I Oppressed?
A Checklist for Testing
Spiritual Bondage

In the progress of the renewal of the redeemed man, it is to the interest of the forces of evil that any element of the fallen life, whether fleshly or soulish, should be kept active, for as the believer becomes "spiritual," he more and more is united in actual spirit-union with the Lord of Glory, and hence more and more escapes the power of evil spirits, and becomes equipped to recognize them and war against them.

—Jessie Penn-Lewis

ONE OF THE MOST FREQUENT THINGS I am asked to do is to test for the possibility of demonic involvement in a Christian's life. The typical phone call goes something like this: "Here's my problem. Nothing else has worked, so could it be of demonic origin?"

If oppression in any form is present in a person's life, you can be sure there's a reason for it. But we often fail to recognize the great variety of possible reasons for our afflictions—everything from sin to chemical imbalance to childhood trauma. I have noticed a troublesome tendency. Novices in spiritual warfare are often too quick to attribute demonic activity to certain symptoms. We need to be careful here.

I have developed a checklist which should be useful both to the Christian who is suffering and to the Christian called upon to help. Discernment involves more than just recognizing the activity of the enemy. It also means understanding the many forms of suffering and affliction which can beset human beings. The more we know about the nature of human vulnerabilities—physical, emotional, and spiritual—the greater chance our discernment will be on target. Accurate discernment is the important first step in spiritual warfare.

ASK FOR DISCERNMENT IN PRAYER

Certain kinds of problems can make us wonder whether demonic involvement may exist. These include: prolonged depression, attacks of fear or anxiety, fearful dreams, compulsive behaviors (anger, sexual bondage, eating disorders), violent thoughts, chemical dependencies, and constant tribulations. When we can't see the cause clearly, we should ask the Lord to remove any oppressive influence that may be present. Sometimes evil spirits will take advantage of an existing physical or emotional problem, and will leave when commanded by a believer acting in faith. After all, the enemy is eager to aggravate our existing agony. Seek help from people you know who are skilled in discernment and prayer, and remember Psalm 34. In our troubles, David exhorts us to extol, praise, and exalt the Lord. To expectantly seek the Lord in the midst of trouble is to place yourself in the position of benefiting from his promise of spiritual help and deliverance.

CONSIDER CAREFULLY OTHER CAUSES
OF YOUR PROBLEM

Do not presume too quickly, on the basis of symptoms or behaviors alone, that afflicting spirits are the cause of your struggle. A whole spectrum of potential causes requires other remedies than deliverance prayer. For example, problem(s) may be rooted in any one or combination of the following factors:

Spiritual

- Unconfessed Sin: you are laboring under the weight of an unclean conscience (Ps 32:1-6).

- Unbelief: weak faith, doublemindedness, doubts, instability that traces back to an uncertainty of your spiritual identity in Christ (Jas 1:6-8).

- Temptations: wrestling with the impulses of the flesh (Gal 5:15, 16).

- Relational Conflicts: hurt, tension, resentment that comes from a refusal to forgive (Eph 4:31, 32).

- Spiritual Starvation: insufficient nourishment, deficient exposure to the Word of God, worship and fellowship (Ps 119:28, 81).

Psychological/Emotional

- Emotional Damage: scars that result from rejection, harsh discipline, a broken home, alcoholic parents, sexual abuse, or negative parenting (fear, guilt, inferiority).

- Psychological Disorders: phobias, anxiety, obsessive-compulsive thoughts and behaviors, clinical depression, character disorders.

Physiological

- Organic Brain Syndromes: epilepsy, senility, Alzheimer's, migraine headaches.

- Biochemical: imbalances of body chemistry, premenstrual syndrome, menopause, postpartum depression, hypoglycemia, diabetes, anxiety disease, allergies, manic-depression, Epstein-Barr virus.

- Stress or Fatigue: consequences of exceeding the laws of nature, including such areas as diet, exercise, and rest.

A number of what I call demonic look-alikes are actually disorders with psychological/emotional or physiological roots. Listed below are examples of problems that should not be quickly labeled demonic. Professional help should be sought out when dealing with these.

- Anxiety Attacks: often anxiety traces to a root cause in one's experience, to a chemical deficiency, or personality disorder. Unexplained, intense fear may feel demonic.

- Clinical Depression: I have often worked with agonized people who thought they were either hopelessly sick, insane, or useless to God because of their depression. *Anyone suffering from prolonged depression should be checked for chemical complications.* Sometimes proper medication can bring remarkable relief and enhance progress in counseling therapy.

- Compulsive Addictions: Primarily alcoholism, drug addiction, sexual compulsions, eating, and gambling disorders. Understandably, the difficulty in finding solutions for these problems leads many to suspect the demonic. It is worth checking, for sometimes demons can gain a foothold here. But these are also behavioral bondages in and of themselves.

- Schizophrenia: Some in deliverance work insist this illness is always of demonic origin. I believe this problem can be caused by a combination of genetic and environmental factors. Paranoia, delusions, and voices are a function of the illness. In some cases, however, evil spirits are also present, adding spiritual affliction to psychiatric suffering. Their expulsion makes the symptoms of the illness more manageable.

- Homosexuality: There is a mistaken tendency to attribute this to demonic influence. On several occasions, I have dealt with spirits that have attached to a person through the practice of a homosexual lifestyle. However, I believe the condition itself traces to personality, parenting, and early peer sexual experience. Sexual preference is not a spirit to be cast out, but a manner of meeting emotional needs that requires deep understanding and healing over time.

- Tourette's Syndrome: Also known as "ticking," this neurological problem prompts a person to utter strange-sounding ticking noises, and often curse words or foul language. At first glance, it seems demonic. But after having worked with several cases, I've realized that the part of the brain that stores negative data is physically affected in this disorder.

Circumstantial

- Personal: Marital or family disharmony, financial stress, personal tragedies, occupational changes, family illnesses.

- Environmental: Factors in our surroundings that affect how we think and feel, such as weather, traffic jams, a depressing television show, and seasonal stresses.

After reviewing the above factors, you may pinpoint one or more factors that may contribute to the problem. If so, pursue a plan to correct the problem. Or, you may determine that none of these factors apply, and that oppression is a possibility.

TRACE THE SOURCE OF OPPRESSION

Identify moral compromises or contacts with persons or places that might have left you open to demonic influence. Demons *may* "hook up" with a person who violates God's law. Typically this happens when someone gets involved in the occult (divination, sorcery, spiritualism, clairvoyance, etc.), holds onto hatred toward another person, practices sexual perversion, or loses control through drugs or alcohol. This kind of demonic attachment can also happen when someone comes into contact with persons or places that may have been "charged" with demonic power (curses or spells may need to be identified and broken). Demonization can also come through violent crimes of rape, attempted murder, sexual abuse, or satanic ritual abuse. A spirit may leave the abuser and attach to the victim. Any ground given to the enemy, either through willful sin, ignorance, or victimization must be removed if a person is to be freed from oppression.

TAKE A LOOK AT FAMILY HISTORY

Identify any persons in your bloodline that may have opened a door to demonic influence. Without conducting a witch-hunt, identify those known to have immoral or idolatrous lifestyles. Also look for prolonged suffering from depression or psychiatric illnesses, and for any instance of suicide. If you are oppressed, you may be encountering the influence of familial spirits that gained entrance into the bloodline at some point. If you are one of the few in your family line who has given your life to Christ, there may be a "river of ungodliness" that flows in your direction. It is appropriate to build a spiritual dam to cut off the effect of the evil of former generations (see the Procedure for Dealing with Generational Sin, Chapter Four).

PRAY WITH FAITH AND AUTHORITY

If the data and your discernment seem to point toward the possibility of oppression, ask the counsel of a trusted friend or pastor. When we pray, God honors our efforts. You may not feel comfortable or qualified to figure this out on your own. Spiritual subtleties cannot be detected by the natural mind. Seek out the assistance of one gifted with spiritual sight. This may not be easy. Look for a deliverance counselor with proven effectiveness, known to be balanced and strong in the Word of God. If one is not available, look for a Christian counselor or therapist open to this dimension. Increasingly, professionals are noting cases of spiritual bondage and are learning the skills of discernment and authoritative prayer.

DISCERNMENT: THE MASTER KEY

Our human condition is indeed a vulnerable one. Body, soul, and spirit interact in complex ways with the world, the flesh, and the devil. Such interactions make for confusing and multilayered difficulties. We need to remember that God is both sovereign *and* omniscient—no matter how confusing things seem to us, *God knows* perfectly, clearly, and totally. And he gives us eyes to see as he sees, and minds to understand as he does, through his gift to us of *discernment*. Spiritual warfare is ineffective and potentially hazardous without discernment, this ability to see where, how, and when God desires to engage the enemy. Keeping this in mind, let us look more closely at the nature of the discernment process itself.

SEVEN

Discernment: Toward a Biblical Definition

But solid food is for the mature, who by constant use have trained themselves to distinguish good from evil. Heb 5:14

SUCCESS IN MINISTRY DEPENDS ON accurately hearing God's voice and discerning his mind. Jesus summed up the guiding principle of his healing ministry, saying that he does only what he sees the Father doing (Jn 5:19). Many servants are quick to say, "Lord, I'll obey you!" But, obey *what*? The moral and redemptive will of God is clear in Scripture, but what does God want me to do in *this* case, in *that* case? How can I know the difference between his thoughts and intentions as distinct from mine, or anyone else's? Learning this can close the gap between my own well-meaning but futile efforts and receiving the empowerment of the Holy Spirit to bear eternal fruit. We all long for this clarity and anointing, to see as God sees and to be about *his* business. To develop a working definition of discernment, it helps to identify *three levels:* the natural ability of *human intuition,* a *general supernatural endowment* available to all believers, and a *specific, sovereign gift* of the discernment of spirits.

HUMAN INTUITION

A friend of mine has an uncanny ability to "read" the character traits of individuals and the social dynamics likely to develop among groups of people. She is not a Christian and does not presume to have any spiritual ability in this regard. But she has reliable perceptive insights that help her know how to avoid involvements with unethical or selfishly motivated people. This capacity to see quickly and keenly behind the outer appearance to capture the quality of a particular person or event is a natural but usually latent human ability. Some people who have developed their skill at reading body language, for example, make great personnel managers and public relations experts. Others are better at analyzing and predicting new trends and function as visionaries in the fields of writing, science, and business. Such perception is a part of the package of human excellence built in by the Creator. When such persons become Christians and receive the Holy Spirit, their natural perceptive ability seems to sharpen significantly.

GENERAL SUPERNATURAL ENDOWMENT

Every person who experiences new birth in Christ undergoes regeneration, an initial and continuing re-creation of the image of Jesus Christ within the personality. This new life is transmitted to the soul by the indwelling of the Spirit (Ti 3:4-7). The Spirit mediates the full grace of the Godhead to the believer and sovereignly helps him or her to operate with specific gifts. One of the abilities given by the Spirit is the capacity to discern good from evil, truth from error. Paul prays for the Philippians:

> And this is my prayer: that your love may abound more and more in knowledge and depth of insight, *so that you may be able to discern what is best and may be pure and blameless* until the day of Christ, filled with the fruit of righteousness that comes through Jesus Christ—to the glory and praise of God. Phil 1:9-11, emphasis mine

General discernment is an endowment of the Holy Spirit to every believer, enabling him or her to perceive personally the grace of God which is available to help the person become holy and avoid evil. The purpose of discernment is to see what God has for us, and to walk in it. It has a practical purpose. Consider the request of the psalmist, "I am your servant; give me discernment that I may understand your statutes" (Ps 119:125). The larger context of Psalm 119 consists of the psalmist's commitment to walk in the ways of the Lord. Proverbs teaches the connection between discretion, understanding, and wisdom. Wisdom, (Hebrew *hokma*) is "living skillfully" in the Lord's way, but first one must *see* and *understand* what the way is in order to choose it! Solomon exhorts the young man: "My son, preserve sound judgment and discernment" (Prv 3:21). The result is that his foot will not stumble by his own walking, nor be snared by the cunning trap of another. The goal of discernment is to enable a person to live a life of godliness.

Within the context of warnings about falling away from faith, the writer of Hebrews spoke of discernment as an element of maturity:

> But solid food is for the mature, who by constant use have trained themselves to distinguish good from evil.
> 5:14

The verb for distinguish is *diakrisin*, which indicates working toward a clear discrimination, a judging by evidence. It encourages me that the verb is preceded by the preposition *pros,* which indicates that the seasoned Christian moves "toward a distinguishing" of good and evil. We have room and time to grow!

A parallel verb used in 1 Corinthians 2:14 sharpens our definition of discernment. Paul states that the things of God are foolishness to the natural man, "and he cannot understand them, because they are spiritually discerned." The verb used here indicates intensive investigation of objects or events. In the context, the spiritual man is enabled by the Spirit to both determine and "understand what God has freely given us" (2:12) for our benefit and blessing. Involved here is a discernment of what is "best, and pure and blameless" for the one seeking to grow in the image of Christ.

In his first epistle, John warns the church of the spirits of anti-Christ that twist and pervert the purity of the gospel with false doctrine. Twice he emphasizes the provision of the Spirit of God: "But you have an anointing from the Holy One, and all of you know the truth" (1 Jn 2:20; cf. 2:27). The anointing serves to reveal the full truth of Jesus Christ to the soul, enabling each believer to detect false teaching and false teachers. Every Christian thus has a certain measure of spiritual discernment and is responsible to test the validity of any spiritual teaching or teacher. You may not be able to decide precisely *what* is wrong, but the Holy Spirit will cause a certain discomfort in your spirit.

For example, your teen may bring home a friend to introduce to you, and you sense a warning in your spirit. It may be specific—you may pick up on a spirit that is deceptive, unclean, or rebellious. Learn to follow these promptings, to pray for protection, and to act if necessary to steer a loved one or friend away from uncomfortable, harmful, or even dangerous situations. Discernment, in the general sense, is God's provision for all believers to guide them in the path of truth and guard their feet from the subtle snares of evil, whether human or demonic. The church must cultivate and use this kind of discernment as society becomes progressively bankrupt at the spiritual level.

SPECIFIC SUPERNATURAL CHARISMA

Beyond the provision of discernment for all believers, is a particular charisma of the Spirit, that "the ability to distinguish between spirits" (1 Cor 12:10), which enables one to accurately detect and distinguish the identities of evil spirits. Not everyone receives this specific grace. The beauty of the body of Christ is that a variety of gifts work together within the body. For the good of all, Christians so gifted must begin to exercise this charisma.

Discerning of spirits consists of spiritual discrimination endowed by the Holy Spirit for the purpose of judging the source of power—human, satanic, or divine. This ability may be immediate, or it may be cultivated over time by observation and by deepening one's sensitivity to the Spirit of God. Picture, if you will, the Holy Spirit as the presence of light that permeates the universe, orchestrating the activity of intelligent, angelic beings who serve as invisible helpers behind the scenes of life. But now imagine the presence of evil spirits, dark malevolent powers who prey upon the masses of mankind. Add to this scenario the constant activity of individual minds and wills of human beings, and you have a mysterious, multilevel interaction of spiritual and social forces that contribute to the flow and fabric of life events.

The Spirit of God, working through the spirit and mind of the Christian, conveys the capacity to detect the source of power. To say that this gift functions only to expose evil spirits limits its scope. I believe it also functions to enable one to "read" the condition of the human spirit, to see through the outer appearance and determine whether the motives of a person are tainted with such things as impurity, deceptiveness, or pride. The goal of the servant of Jesus is to see as Jesus sees. John recorded an interesting description of Jesus' discernment: "many people saw the miraculous signs he was doing and believed in his name. But Jesus would not entrust himself to them, for *he knew all men*" (Jn 2:23, 24, emphasis mine).

His eyes looked past the faces, through the facades, and saw the spirit. With this capability, the discerner of spirits learns to determine the inner source of any outer manifestation. Some people function better in perceiving the corruption of the human spirit, others are more effective in detecting evil spirits.

A sense of our own inadequacy is usually what drives us to actively acknowledge the Holy Spirit's presence and to expect the manifestation of his gifts. This, in turn, leads to a measurable increase in the sharpness of discernment and effectiveness in counseling. To describe *how* discernment works, I offer the following equation:

Holy Spirit
▲
  Inward Impression
  ▲
     REASONED OBSERVATION = DISCERNMENT
   ◁
  Outward Manifestation
◁
Human or Demonic Spirit

Impression is the inward communication of truth imparted by the Spirit. Manifestation is the outward activity or reaction of a human or evil spirit. Reasoned observation is the process in the mind that weighs all data and arrives at a Spirit-guided conclusion. A dual process exists in which the person listens both to the Spirit and carefully watches what happens outwardly to others. Effectiveness will increase when a person learns to distinguish the promptings of the Spirit from his or her own human thoughts and impulses. Spiritual growth in the gift of discernment is primarily gained by faithfully following Christ and, secondarily, by talking with others about how it works.

Paul's encounter with Elymas the magician in Acts 13:4-12 powerfully illustrates the gift of discernment. The sorcerer opposed Paul and Barnabas' efforts to share the gospel with the proconsul Sergius Paulus. Inspired by the Spirit, Paul discerned judgment from the Lord and called Elymas a "child of the devil . . . an enemy of everything that is right . . . full of all kinds of deceit and trickery." The magician was then stricken with temporary blindness. It might be appropriate to take Paul's lead today in exposing the truth-twisting of false teachers and practitioners of occultism. Such power encounters, if entered into under God's directive, would bear great fruit. Our pluralistic culture is far too apologetic when it comes to blatant deception and perversity. It is time to blow the whistle on darkness and wrongdoing.

Let me comment on the corollary gifts of knowledge and wisdom. A word of knowledge usually consists of specific information from the Holy Spirit that is related to the salvation, healing, or deliverance of a person. Jesus' remarkable knowledge about the woman at the well (Jn 4:17) illustrates this. He *knew* specific things about her. Similarly, I have been in ministry settings where words, thoughts, or impressions came to mind, revealing needed information about the person seeking help or about the source of bondage. This is a word from God *about* a specific person or situation.

Wisdom is counsel or insight from God about the

underlying nature of a difficult situation or personal problem. Wisdom increases your understanding not only of the problem at hand, but also of God's heart and mind, and the mysteries of his kingdom and work among men. Often wisdom comes with a word from Scripture that, when spoken, has immediate relevance and potency.

Each of these gifts must be tested. At times the message or prompting from God may be mixed with the motivations of the man involved in its delivery. In order for these gifts to function properly, there must be accountability, the testing of their truthfulness. Only in the context of church authority can the gifts operate free of human corruption or demonic counterfeit. Whenever possible, deliverance should be conducted by a team. Many inaccurate inspirations and misguided directives could be avoided if this kind of accountability were built into the practice of the power gifts.

THE QUESTION OF QUALIFICATION

Ideally, the ability to operate under the anointing of the Holy Spirit should result from a life dedicated to Christ, a life daily open to the grace which molds heart and mind. Spiritual maturity should parallel the manifestation of spiritual power. Even so, it always amazes me that God still pours his power through flawed vessels. A man may struggle with personal pride, anger, sexual fantasies, and still find that God chooses to use him in the work of his kingdom. If we all waited until the wrinkles were smoothed out, no one would be left for God to use. God employs imperfect people as his instruments. Still, growth in the image of Jesus must be primary and using his gifts secondary. The standard of holiness must be upheld. For even if there are measurable results of ministry, a man or woman of flawed character may bring dishonor to the Lord's name and may discredit the results in the eyes of others.

Although all Christians can cultivate spiritual discernment skills, some are given discernment as a specific gifting of the Spirit.

Those gifted with discernment need one important qualification: the ability to humbly depend on God. They need to learn how to wait on the Lord and watch for his signals. Pride and presumption must be nailed to the Cross. The discerner of spirits must perpetually be a humble learner, one motivated by the compassion of Jesus. Anyone who operates with spiritual sight can easily be tempted by pride, criticism, and judgment. For example, you might discern an area of sin or weakness in a pastor's or leader's life. How easy to think, "Lord, look at that! How can so-and-so possibly presume to be a leader? What are you going to do about this?" True discernment always operates with God's own love, mercy, and patience, as well as with his power. As with every other spiritual gift, discernment is not *ours* but *God's*. Our eyes may indeed be open to see reality, but only God can deal with that reality, in his way, in his time. May God grant to those enabled to see as he sees the capacity to trust him to bring timely resolution to the problems he has enabled them to perceive.

EIGHT

Establishing Your Home as a Spiritual Refuge

As the mountains surround Jerusalem,
So the Lord surrounds his people both now and
*   forevermore.*
*   the scepter of the wicked will not remain*
*   over the land allotted to the righteous,*
*   for then the righteous might use their hands to do*
*   evil.*   Ps 125:2, 3

PROVERBS TELLS US THAT "he who fears the Lord has a secure fortress, and for his children it will be a refuge." What, precisely, is "it"? Surely not a castle, nor a guaranteed income, nor unlimited medical benefits. "It" is the "fear of the Lord." The fortress is the rooting of one's life in the faithfulness of God. When everything in this world crumbles and collapses, unshakable trust in God's goodness is the only source of peace. One of the most important truths we can draw from Scripture is that God himself is "home," he alone is a refuge and the place of repose for the human soul. When life is normal, this truth can be hard to remember. Often it takes tragedy, trial, and distress to shake us loose from earthly security and compel us to take refuge in the Lord.

THE QUESTION OF PROTECTION

Most of us are familiar with the promises of Psalm 91, beginning with verse 1: "He who dwells in the shelter of the Most High will rest in the shadow of the Almighty." The psalmist enumerates the ways and means of God's protection: safety from the snare, from pestilence, night terrors, and enemy arrows. The strongest statement takes the form of a conditional promise:

> If you make the Most High your dwelling—even the LORD, who is my refuge—then no harm will befall you, no disaster will come near your tent. For he will command his angels concerning you to guard you in all your ways. vs. 9-11

The "If-Then" seems straightforward enough. God is said to "command" his angels to guard the righteous in "all ways." " 'Because he loves me,' says the LORD, 'I will rescue him; I will protect him, for he acknowledges my name' " (vs. 14). How much comfort and assurance *can* be drawn from such passages? Does this psalm contain a theology of protection, or is the psalmist simply expressing poetic optimism? Whenever I think of the question of spiritual protection, I am also reminded of Paul's assertion: "But the Lord is faithful, and he will strengthen and protect you from the evil one" (2 Thes 3:3). My purpose is not to explain the mystery of suffering, but to explore some observations related to spiritual warfare.

Most of us realize that bad things do happen to good people. All of us know of people who fit the "Job syndrome," those who endure unbearable trials. We look about and see folks just like us suffering the ravages of cancer. Some of our friends have been taken advantage of by unscrupulous business partners. The universe is a risky place to live!

Contingency is built into the creation. We battle bacteria and viruses, a natural order that threatens us with calamity, sinful people who can harm us, and invisible demonic beings. Our greatest comfort comes from Romans 8:28: "And we know that in all things God works for the good of those who love him, who have been called according to his purpose." "All things" may *not* be good. No sane person would ever call rape or murder "good." But the passage affirms that every event can be turned to an eternally good purpose by God our Redeemer.

If we wholeheartedly seek to "remain" in loving relationship with the Lord and allow his words to "remain" in us (Jn 15:7), then we are walking "in the shadow" of his will. The other half of Paul's assurance in 2 Thessalonians 3:4 reads, "We have confidence in the Lord that you are doing and will continue to do the things we command." Protection from the evil one depends upon commitment to follow truth. John makes the same point in his epistle (1 Jn 5:18). When I walk in the truth, whatever comes to me is either ordained or allowed by God. He always has the option to miraculously intervene. He can and probably often does command angels to protect those who belong to him. Why one person is called to endure a tragedy and another is delivered from it remains a mystery.

How can we reconcile the promises of Psalm 91 to reality? If we seek to *abide* in vital union with the Lord and to *acknowledge* him in the circumstances of life, then we *are* in his will. We *are* held in the hollow of his hand. No coincidental harm will touch us. We need to trust that God is in touch with the daily events of our lives, working as a loving craftsman to fashion goodness out of grief. The difficulty here is that we cannot see past the veil that divides this life from the next. "For we know in part and prophesy in part" until the perfection comes and we perceive all of reality as it is (1 Cor 13:9). Until that time, we are sustained by our faith, hope, and love.

THE PROMISE OF THE PRESENCE

A fallen world permeated with invisible spiritual warfare offers no guarantees of physical safety. But we do have a scriptural guarantee that the Almighty is present in all events of life. Whether or not we can perceive the divine presence, we have the promise that through the peaks and valleys, the Lord is there. God gave this assurance to Moses (Ex 33:14), to Joshua (Jos 1:5, 9), Gideon (Jgs 6:12), and to all the prophets. The Father of Israel spoke through Isaiah: "Fear not, for I have redeemed you; I have called you by name; you are mine." He assured Israel of his presence in passing through the waters and through the fire: *"Do not be afraid, for I am with you"* (Is 43:1-5). It's no coincidence that Jesus reiterated this same promise: "Surely I am with you always, to the very end of the age" (Mt 28:20; cf. 18:20). Most of the time, we have to take this promise on faith, but sometimes special moments of grace assure us that this presence is palpably real. We can cultivate spiritual disciplines that enhance the perception of God's presence and release his power in greater measure.

A friend from Taiwan shared such an experience. Wife

of the director of a Bible College and Lay Training Institute, Lana was often left with the children for long periods of time to maintain her home as a haven of rest and protection. During the local "ghost festival," when people made offerings to appease the hungry spirits of those who had died in tragic accidents, Lana often sensed an oppressive presence in their home. During those times, she felt threatened and vulnerable. She would also notice heightened agitation among the children. Restless sleep and exhaustion accompanied these times.

As Lana and her husband read and studied more about signs and symptoms of demonic activity, the Holy Spirit gave discernment and prompted them to move in authority to counteract the darkness. They went through their home, consecrating it to God and his use, and commanding any evil spirits encroaching on their territory to depart. They prayed for the children, and for one another, applying the power of Jesus' blood. This represented a definite turning point. Both of them experienced a freshness of the Lord's presence in and about them. You may ask, was the Lord not there before this? Of course he was. But he has told us about the battle and has given us weapons. We are supposed to call on his name in the midst of trouble, and to act with the authority Jesus gives to every believer.

In practicing God's presence, we need to understand some implications of the New Covenant. After that, we can discuss practical steps toward establishing our homes as places of spiritual refuge.

UNDERSTANDING GOD'S COVENANTS

The Lord's desire has always been to draw near to his people. In the Old Covenant, his presence and power were manifested through particular places or persons. The most dramatic examples are the pillar of fire and the column of smoke in the wilderness and the *shekinah* glory above the Ark of the Covenant. At various times, the Lord chose prophets, judges, kings, and priests to serve as vessels to mediate his presence. The Spirit would come upon a man or a woman, prompting that person to speak as God would speak, and act as he would act. At the center of the Old Covenant relationship with Israel was God's presence in the temple, in the Holy of Holies. It was here that the consecrated priest met God.

In the New Covenant, the Christian receives the very life of God and becomes a "temple of the Holy Spirit" (1 Cor 6:19). What an incredible and marvelous mystery God's plan is! Somehow the Divine One places a part of his person into those chosen and foreordained to be conformed to the image of his Son. And so the church becomes a "dwelling in which God lives by his Spirit" (Eph 2:22). The very Source of life chooses a people so that he can "live with them and walk among them" (2 Cor 6:16). As partakers of the divine nature, as temples in whom God has chosen to dwell, Christians mediate the presence of the Most High. Paul affirms that God "through us spreads everywhere the fragrance of the knowledge of him" (2 Cor 2:14). Therefore, those places where we live and work should be dedicated as God's holy domain, endowed with the power of his presence, and used for his redemptive purposes. I'm not speaking metaphorically. The Christian is a walking temple! And the presence that flows from the Christian is the light and love of Yahweh himself.

One's home can be an oasis of the Lord's presence, available for spiritual refuge, family worship, the nurture and instruction of children, and witness to unbelievers. A blessing extends to the dwelling of the righteous:

The LORD's curse is on the house of the wicked,
but he blesses the home of the righteous. Prv 3:33

The blessing extends first to *persons* in the family, and also to the *place* of habitation. On our wedding invitation, my wife Terri and I penned the little phrase, "As Christ Is at Home in Our Hearts, He Will Be at the Heart of Our Home." Is the Lord Jesus welcome and restfully at home in all the rooms of your heart?

STEPS IN ESTABLISHING A SPIRITUAL REFUGE

Wherever Christians are—at home, in an office, at a campsite, a camper on the road, or a motel room—should be an oasis of God's presence, a shelter of protection from demonic interference and the evil deeds of men and women. The Lord has destined us, through the resurrection of Jesus, to fulfill the mandate given Adam to be co-regents on earth, mediating his authority. Where do we begin?

Remove Desecration. Evil spirits can pollute places with their unholy presence. Such demonization usually occurs when mortal beings commit immoral acts that open the door to the activity of demons. For example, a house used for the manufacture or selling of drugs, a place used for prostitution, or a building used by a fortune-teller or spiritualist group may invite demons of bondage, deception, violence, lust, sexual perversion, or familiar spirits of the occult. Even when the perpetrators have left the scene, evil spirits may linger, hoping to prey upon unsuspecting newcomers.

When you purchase a used home, lease office space, rent a house, or spend a night in a hotel room or condominium, you should cleanse that place from the lingering effects of sin and wickedness. Lest I invite fanaticism here, let me state a guiding principle: follow the discernings and promptings of the Spirit.

Consider some inspiring biblical precedents. King Asa, a man who "did what was right in the eyes of the Lord" (2 Kgs 15:11) drove the shrine prostitutes out of Israel, removed the idols, cut down the Asherah poles, and even had the courage to depose his grandmother Maacah from her position as "Queen Mother" of the fertility cult. We know of Elijah's confrontation with the prophets of Baal. Less familiar are the reforms of King Josiah: "Josiah got rid of the mediums and spiritists, the household gods, the idols and all the other detestable things seen in Judah and Jerusalem" (2 Kgs 23:24).

Consecrate and Dedicate the Place to God. Set your home or place of work apart for God's use. Release your rights to your property. Offer the place to God, inviting his presence. Verbal, visible pronouncement is important in declaring this intention. The head of the household should lead in a prayer of dedication (Jos 24:15). Solomon's prayer of dedication of the temple, though lengthy, may serve as another model for this (2 Chr 6). A word for single parent mothers—*you* can take this role for your home and children and establish the Lord's authority over the place he has provided. You may wish to ask your pastor or a friend to perform such a dedication, but be aware that God will honor *your* faith and prayer.

Sample Prayer for Dedication of a Home

Father, I call to you in Jesus' name and in the power of your Holy Spirit. You are the Lord of my life and of this place. I ask that you would search out and bring into the light any unconfessed sin or act of wickedness committed in this place. I apply the blood of Jesus Christ to break the power of enemy spirits attached to this home. Lord, by the power of the Cross, and the truth of your word, I ask you to move on my behalf to cleanse this place of all evil.

Lord, fill my home with your holy presence. Use it for your purposes. Set your watching angels at the boundaries of this property to shield and protect us from evil, according to your Word (Jn 17:15; 2 Thes 3:3). I proclaim that the power of the evil one has no place here. Through the name that is above every name, the King of Kings and Lord of Lords.

Honor the Lord. Fill your home with objects and activities that bring glory to God. In a prophecy spoken against the house of Eli, the Lord said, "Those who honor me I will honor, but those who despise me will be disdained" (1 Sm 2:30). A tangible blessing extends to the family and the dwelling of the one who honors God. Let's be practical. When you decorate your house or office, remember that what the eye sees, the mind and heart will follow. Consider tastefully including paintings, plaques, books, missionary prayer maps, and Christian symbols that catch the eye and direct the mind toward God. Regular times of reading God's Word should form the cornerstone of family devotional life. Families, couples, and singles living together should learn to gather regularly to pray and praise.

The Lord had reasons for instituting the feasts and festivals of the Old Covenant. Many were object lessons of the eternal truths of the Word and ways of God. As New Covenant Christians, saved and sustained by grace, we can celebrate some of these observances in light of New Testament revelation. A blessing awaits those who observe a Sabbath, a Passover feast, or Pentecost. Focusing on the continuity of God's truth honors him and establishes our homes as places devoted to his purpose.

Maintain Protection. For your house to be a spiritual refuge you must understand that you have an ongoing duty to discern and pray for the protection of home and family.

Pray unceasingly with alertness: It is nearly impossible to be in a continual state of prayer that is conscious and verbal. What Paul means (1 Thes 5:17) is to maintain sensitive communion with the Spirit, being open to his promptings. We can trust our indwelling guide to signal us when spiritual danger is imminent.

Exercise spiritual authority: So many failures to appropriate God's power occur precisely at this point. A word to husbands and fathers: decide to get over your hesitation about exercising headship in your home. The smallest initiative here will result in God's blessing. Wives, back off a bit if necessary to allow your husband to involve the family in prayer. The Lord is looking for men who honor him and who take headship seriously.

Discern and deal with evil influences: Be cautious about inviting strangers into your home: parents should be careful about who comes through the door. Carefully check out your babysitters. Instruct your children to ask, "Who's there?" before opening the door in your absence. Second, John 10 indicates a word of caution concerning spiritual influences that might come knocking at your door.

Confront ungodly values: Talk to your children about the difference between Christian values and those of the world. Elementary school age children are not too young to start learning this. At the appropriate time, talk straightforwardly about premarital sex, drug use, occultism, political corruption, and covetousness, the effects of heavy metal music, and content in television and movies. Don't terrify them, but make sure they're informed when they need to be. Fathers must especially define values and exercise wise spiritual authority when children violate these values. Improper attitudes, such as disrespect, rebellion, and deceit must be recognized and dealt with. As Christian parents you need to recognize that a concerted assault is being made on the hearts and minds of your children. Satan has a strategy to divert them from God and lead them into destruction. A godly lifestyle in the home can protect children.

Resolve family tensions: Ephesians 4:27 could not be clearer! Deal with attitudes of resentment, anger, and bitterness before the devil gets an opportunity to deal with you. How many times after an argument have you tried to settle into peaceful sleep without mending the rift with your mate, parent, or friend? Even if you think yourself free of guilt, you still may need to go to the other party and talk it out. Being convinced you are "right" doesn't produce peace! God wants us to live in harmony, to reconcile conflicts with truthfulness and love. Whenever this is not done, consequences ensue: lack of peace in the home, stress on the mind and body, and an open door for potential oppression.

Deal with isolated attacks: You may discern that an arrow of evil has slipped into your home or family life. Ask and trust the Spirit to give you more discernment about it. You may be experiencing a barrage of fear during the night, heavy discouragement, or intense strife. Your teen may be moving with a rebellious crowd and bringing a spirit into the home. You may have watched an "out of bounds" television program that seems to open your mind to spiritual oppression. Learn to discern and deal with these events quickly and decisively. Our tardiness in responding will keep us in the fog longer than we need to be. The devil may have nothing directly to do with the problem, but call on the Lord for help and assert his authority. To do this is simply to exercise faith.

Establish Godly Heritage. The refuge you are establishing has exciting ramifications for your children and their children after them. We have the privilege of dedicating our lineage to the Lord. Psalm 102:28 says: "The children of your servants will live in your presence; their descendants will be established before you." And Psalm 103:17, 18 says: "The LORD's love is with those who fear him, and his righteousness with their children's children—with those who keep his covenant and remember to obey his precepts." My wife and I have learned to pray regularly for our children's mates, their choice of friends, their selection of a career. Standing on these Scriptures, we are believing God for his best for them, and for their offspring.

As usual, however, there *is* a catch! As husband and father, I need to keep the faith, but grandchildren who come under the blessing of my prayers need to make their own choice to "keep his covenant." Our faithfulness and prayers can establish a track, a momentum of God's blessing that will provide hidden strength to those who follow. Such prayers are investments that grow with compound interest. The maturity date may be far off. But someone who may never know you prayed will reap a blessed benefit!

SHELTERS IN THE STORM

Being a vessel for God's presence enables you to bless others with his strength and healing. It enables you to establish a witness for those who don't know Christ. On the natural level, things look bleak. Raising godly children in a perverse generation is a challenge. On the supernatural level, however, God stands ready to pour out his presence upon those who have the courage to take his Word seriously and stand on the truth.

Spiritual authority is not reserved for elder statesmen of the faith: for our pastors, elders, and missionaries. Spiritual discernment and the practice of authority are gifts to every believer. It is time to fight for the peace and blessing of God in our families and for the values of his kingdom. It is time to use the sword of the Spirit to drive the devil away from our homes, businesses, and churches. In the midst of filth and the fallenness, God calls us to establish an oasis of his healing presence, where the water of life may be freely available for both saint and sinner. We can all catch this vision: our home as a spiritual refuge conveying the peace and mercy of God to those in desperate need of it.

NINE

Patterns for Effectual Prayer

Exercising our authority in Jesus' name, our Scepter,
may go beyond merely asking our Lord to grant a
particular request. It may mean we actually command
a situation to change in Jesus' name simply because
Christ has already given us that authority. He said,
"Whoever says to this mountain, 'Be removed' . . .
and does not doubt in his heart . . . he shall have
whatever he says" (Mk 11:23).

—Jack Hayford
and Dick Eastman

THE MORE CLOSELY I WALK WITH JESUS, the more sensitive I will be to his promptings to pray "in his name." The walk of the disciple becomes a constant prayer. This is what Paul meant by the phrase "to pray without ceasing," watching for the word and way of God in every circumstance. Most of the time, such prayer involves having a general awareness of the Lord in our thoughts and circumstances. We go about our duties and tasks aware that we are in him and he in us. But there are also special times of concerted focus. When we set our hearts to seek him, we bring praise, offer petitions, and seek specific help. In this chapter, we will outline some effective responses to various aspects of the battles we face.

I have no interest in providing pat formulas for spiritual success. The Lord is our success. No power is intrinsic to the words or order of words in the prayers that follow. I only mean to suggest that I have observed certain guidelines for effectual prayer, with exciting results. Our Lord can do whatever he wants whenever he wants. But he has given prayer to his church as a high and holy privilege. Through prayer, we get to know him, his word, his ways. We learn how to ask, how to hear his voice, how to receive his answers. Receiving what God wants for us enables us to grow up into the fullness of the stature of Jesus, available to him as ambassadors, anointed with his authority.

It takes a lifetime to learn the ways of God. To learn to "ask anything according to his will" and to "have what we asked of him" (1 Jn 5:14, 15) presumes a certain quality and quantity of time spent with him. And so we see the disciples asking Jesus, "Lord, teach us to pray." Not *how* to pray, but simply *to* pray! Through the practice comes the perfecting. By entering the practice of the prayers provided here, you will give the Lord opportunity to demonstrate his faithfulness to respond to Jesus' priestly petition: "My prayer is not that you take them out of the world but that you protect them from the evil one" (Jn 17:15). Prayer that is Christ-centered, faith-filled, and anointed with authority will release the hand of the Father to accomplish his purposes.

WARFARE PRAYER AND RESISTANCE: SPECIALIZED FORMATS

The prayers that follow are simplified, patterned approaches to general categories of spiritual warfare. My purpose here is to present a generalized picture of how resistance against the devil should look. Each person and each situation is different, so it is essential to follow the promptings of the Spirit.

Understand as well that two distinct dimensions are involved in this type of prayer: first, there is communion with the Lord and petition offered to him and, second, there is resistance, the authoritative *rebuke*, directed at Satan and his forces. These two radically different functions go side-by-side. We draw strength and inspiration from prayer, and then we allow the Spirit to anoint truth as arrows against the lies of the devil. This is precisely what Jesus did in the wilderness temptation. Drawing vertically from his relationship with the Father, he horizontally unraveled Satan's deception with a verbal rebuke. We *pray* to God, motivated by a desire to draw near to him. We *resist* Satan, motivated by a holy hatred of evil.

Isolated Spiritual Attack. Have you ever felt yourself to be targeted by demonic forces? At times, the evil spirits that indwell or surround the ungodly may see the life of Christ in you and react with hostility.

Every day we interact with neighbors or fellow employees who dabble in metaphysics or who are living immoral lifestyles. A boss or supervisor who knows your Christian identity can make life miserable. If the Lord helps you see that a real spiritual power is working behind these things, use the following approach.

Prayer During Attack

Heavenly Father, you are my Refuge and my Rock. You are in control of everything that happens in my life. I am your servant, called by your name. Thank you for giving me the helmet of salvation—my identity in your Son is secure. Nothing can separate me from your love.

Thank you for forgiving and cleansing my guilt (proceed with any confession that might be needed). I put on your breastplate of righteousness. Holy Spirit, search out and bring into the light any schemes of darkness directed at me. I take up the shield of faith to stand against the works of the evil one. In Jesus' name, I stand on the truth of the Word of God: "The reason the Son of God appeared was to destroy the devil's work" (1 Jn 3:8).

Resistance

Satan, I rebuke you in the authority of Jesus Christ. I declare your works in my life destroyed. Jesus triumphed over you in the wilderness, on the Cross, and in the grave. His resurrection has sealed your fate. I triumph over you now in the strength of his name. I resist and rebuke your efforts to oppress, afflict, or deceive me. I remove from you the right to rob me of the joy and fruit of my salvation. Through the power of the blood of Calvary, I command all powers of darkness assigned to me, sent to me, or surrounding me now, to leave. Go where Jesus Christ orders you to go, never to return.

Protection. It is always appropriate to seek the Lord for his protection. If you are involved at some level with spiritual warfare, these types of prayer should become a regular part of your spiritual discipline. You should confidently apply the potency of Jesus' prayer to your own life, your home, children, vehicles, fellow workers, missionaries, and the pastoral staffs of your local churches.

Prayer for Protection

Lord, your Word declares that you will shield and protect your children from the power of the evil one (Ps

97:10; Jn 17:15; 2 Thes 3:3). You are *El Elyon,* the Most High God, sovereign Lord of all things visible and invisible. Everything is in your hand. I ask you, in the name of Jesus, to shield _____ with the presence of your Spirit (Ps 3:3). May your glory follow after _____ as a rear guard (Is 58:8). Lord, be a refuge to _____. Support him or her with your everlasting arms, and drive the enemy away (Dt 33:27). Assign and send your holy angels to protect and deliver your servant from danger (Pss 34:7; 91:9-11). I commend _____ to your watchful care. I ask that no purpose of yours be thwarted by the interference of Satan and his forces (Jb 42:2). Father, in accordance with Jesus' prayer, deliver _____ from all evil.

Prayer for the Protection of Children

Father, you alone are my refuge, my strength, my fortress. I ask you to honor your Word and be a refuge to my family (Prv 14:26). I ask you, through Jesus' intercession, to grant to us your sovereign protection from evil. Show me any sin or disobedience that robs me and my family of your protection (1 Jn 5:18). Show me, Holy Spirit, anything that grieves your blessing in our lives (Eph. 4:30).

I entrust my children to you. They are your gifts to me. I ask you to surround _____ with your presence, and to shield him or her from Satan's power. God, shed your light upon your servants, bathe us with the joy of your redemption (Ps 97:11). Cover _____ with the power of the blood of your Son (Rv 12:11). I ask you, Father, to expose and destroy schemes of the enemy planned against _____ and to assign your holy angels to guard and protect him or her, according to your perfect will (Ps 91:11-13; Mt 18:10; Heb 1:14). Lord

Jesus, thank you for praying for our protection. By faith I receive your protection for my family.

Cleansing a Place. Places, as well as persons, may be polluted by demonic presence. Any believer with minimal discernment can detect the "dirty" atmosphere of a pornographic adult bookstore, the eerie feeling of the New Age occult bookstore, or the heavy and fearful atmosphere of a prison environment. Occasionally, you might find yourself in a motel room or other temporary residence that feels like anything but a refuge.

Sometimes when we find ourselves in evil territory, a defensive posture is appropriate. We are stepping into the enemy's camp, and unless directed to do something, we should simply stand firm and shield ourselves. At other times, it may be wise to pray through and cleanse the atmosphere of any motel room or used home that we inhabit for any length of time. Let's not be fanatical about this. It is not always necessary. But if the Holy Spirit should prompt you in the midst of a miserable night's rest, go for it.

Prayer of Cleansing

Lord, I claim this place for your purposes. I stand on the truth of your Word: "The scepter of the wicked will not remain over the land allotted to the righteous" (Ps. 125:3). I believe you have given me this place (home, business, motel room, condo). I dedicate it to you, and ask you to fill it with your holy presence. I separate myself from any iniquity that has occurred here in past times. I apply the power of Jesus' blood to remove any desecration of God's name in this place. I ask you, in Jesus' authority, to set watching angels around this property, protecting your servant from the work of the evil one. (If this is a hotel or motel room, I will add the following:) Father, I ask for your holy presence and holy angels to linger here, to touch the lives of those who inhabit the room after me. Bring conviction to their hearts, and draw them to seek after you.

Resistance

I stand on the authority of the Lord Jesus Christ, whose name is above every name, to weaken the power of evil in this place. Through the blood of Christ, I remove all desecration of the name of God that was prompted either by human or demonic beings. I command all enemies of Jesus Christ that have access to this place, or who may be here now . . . to leave. Go now where you are ordered to go, by the voice of the Holy Spirit. I claim this property for the kingdom of light. I order all darkness to flee, in the name of Jesus the King.

Breaking Curses. Occasionally we may experience demonic assaults that originate from curses spoken by those who oppose us. Ignorance and naivete can make us vulnerable.

A tribal language worker in Bogota, Colombia told me this story. The worker had visited a certain tribe on an exploratory mission. At about 4:00 A.M. she was awakened by a pressure around her throat. Though fearful and laboring for breath, she committed her cause to the Lord, rebuked the enemy, and settled back to sleep. Two days later she met the tribal medicine man. He spoke to her through a translator: "I was not able to harm you. Why?" She took this opportunity to share the Lord with him, and spoke God's blessing on his life. Several days after this, the shaman received Christ into his life.

Prayer for Breaking Curses

Lord Jesus, you have called and equipped me to follow you and to do your will. I submit to you. In my affliction, I ask you to convict me of any sin that allows the arrows of Satan to buffet me. I am willing and ready to repent of anything that gives the enemy a place. I ask you to reveal areas of ignorance or fear that may have given the enemy opportunity. Lord, search out, expose, and break the power of all schemes of Satan that have been sent to me. I seek your face—I call to you. Hear and answer my prayer, and deliver me from this trouble. I ask you to turn this evil into good.

Resistance

Satan, I raise my shield of faith against you and resist you with the sword of the Holy Spirit, the Word of God that proclaims your judgment as a false god, an accuser and afflictor of the sons of the Almighty. I announce your works in my life (and in the life of my family, team members, disciples, etc.) destroyed. Through the power of the blood of Jesus Christ, I refuse and break all evil curses, hexes, vexes, spells, incantations, rituals, psychic powers, or works of witchcraft sent to defeat or destroy my life and ministry. I resist all demonic powers sent to me from _____ (identify any witch, occult practitioner, shaman, tribal chief, religious leader, etc.). I command all powers of evil to return immediately to the source from which you came. In the name of Jesus, I speak blessing on _____ (the one who has cursed you). I send the Holy Spirit to you to convict you of your sin, and draw you into the light. I call you to turn from your sin and turn to the mercy of the living God.

Proverbs 26:2 gives comfort to the soldier of the cross: "Like a fluttering sparrow or a darting swallow, an undeserved curse does not come to rest." Walk in the spirit, walk in the whole counsel of God, live a life of faith, and your shield will be in place.

ADOPTED CHILDREN

Many Christians choose to adopt children. In some cases, bringing an adopted child into a home can cause unusual tension. Naturally, the adopted child must make psychological adjustments, but spiritual influences may also be at work. Demonic activity may trace back into family history, or to the circumstances surrounding the conception of the child. A parent, pastor, or counselor may pray and expect God to break any bondage. Prayer may also be offered while a child is sleeping or being held.

Prayer for Adopted Children

Father, I call to you in Jesus' name on behalf of _____. In your mercy, Lord, I ask you to search out and expose any unconfessed sin in _____'s blood ancestry that gives the devil any advantage. I take legal authority in Jesus Christ to forsake this sin (be specific, if possible, *e.g.*, incest, hate, murder, witchcraft) and to separate _____ from Satan's accusation. "The reason the Son of God appeared was to destroy the devil's works." I proclaim the works of the devil exposed and destroyed in _____'s life (observe the child's response as you pray—prevail until you perceive that the child is peaceful, calm, and resting securely. If there is a manifestation, command the spirits to depart. Close your prayer by speaking a scriptural blessing on the child.)

For children six years of age or older, it may be necessary to verify the child's personal commitment to Christ and enlist his or her moral cooperation in your efforts. Deal with unconfessed sin that may give the enemy ground. Explain why you are praying. Do not pray openly if it stirs fear or misunderstanding. Observe any facial or behavioral responses to your efforts. Pause and ask for feedback, *i.e*, impressions, feelings, bodily sensations that may confirm what the Lord is doing. For adolescents and teens, you should follow deliverance procedures outlined for adults.

Praying for the Lost. Can you do spiritual warfare on behalf of unbelievers? In a very real sense, the lost are held hostage to the blinding and binding influence of the evil one. In the parable of the seed and sower, Jesus depicts the demons who rob people of the ability to understand the truth as the "birds of the air" that steal the seed. Paul says: "The god of this age has blinded the minds of unbelievers, so that they cannot see the light of the gospel of the glory of Christ" (2 Cor 4:4). And John tells us that "the whole world is under the control of the evil one" (1 Jn 5:19). In his wrath against God, Satan satiates his anger by dragging to hell as many souls as he can grab. Hostages do not set themselves free. A rescue is required. How can we cooperate with the Holy Spirit in seeing the bondage of unbelief broken?

In our burden for the lost, we must understand a vital truth spoken by Jesus: "This is the verdict: Light has come into the world, but men loved darkness instead of light because their deeds were evil" (Jn 3:19). Each man and woman makes a choice to seek light or to serve self. Apart from the movement of the individual will to seek the grace of God, our prayers cannot and will not wrench someone free from the grip of sin and the power of Satan.

But we may still pray in conformity to God's will, who "wants all men to be saved and to come to a knowledge of the truth" (1 Tm 2:4). Peter tells us that he is "not wanting anyone to perish, but everyone to come to repentance" (2 Pt 3:9). Doctrinal issues of election and free will aside, I believe we must pray in confidence for the salvation of each person God brings across our path. If this is God's heart, it must be ours as well. Our role is simply to help another say yes to the conviction of the Holy Spirit and the grace of God offered in Christ. We need to petition the Lord for opportunities to share the Word with those for whom pray. Then, we wait, watch, and follow the Spirit's prompting, always being "prepared to give an answer" (1 Pt 3:15) to a seeking soul. The following petition can be prayed as a silent, focused prayer on behalf of the unsaved person. It is most effective to pray this in the presence of the person, even while involved in friendly contact or conversation.

Prayer for Conversion of Unbelievers

Father, I bring to you my burden for _____. I claim him or her for salvation. Lord, it is your desire that _____ not perish. Holy Spirit, make Jesus known to _____. Stir within this person the desire to seek salvation and convict him or her of sin. Lord, soften any resistance to the truth, and plant seeds of the word in this person's mind and heart. Lord, break his or her will. Make this person desperate. Bring _____ to the end of himself or herself.

Lord, I ask you to break Satan's power in _____'s

life. Spirit of Jesus, silence and subdue the voice of the enemy. In the authority of Christ, I weaken any strongholds in _____'s life. Holy Spirit, move in your power to separate away from this person the influence of unclean spirits, and stir him or her to repentance. I bind the power of any spirits of confusion and unbelief that blind the mind. Lord, enable him or her to hear your Word with clarity. Send someone to share a word of testimony.

If a person makes a decision to receive and to follow Jesus, it is wise to "close the doors" to Satan's prior influence, once and for all. The new believer is rescued from the dominion of darkness and brought into the kingdom of the Son (Col 1:13), and thus inherits the assurance of eternal identity in Christ. But unless the power of Satan is broken, a convert may still face some real hassle. The devil does not give up without a fight. In conjunction with a prayer of repentance and the receiving of salvation, a severing of Satan's influence should also occur. The person should destroy all occultic books and objects and sever any ties that would carry bondage to the old life. Use discretion with this prayer—it may not be necessary. For most folks, the main bondages are those of sin and self.

Prayer for the New Convert

Father, thank you for your gift of salvation. Thank you for setting me free and for delivering my life from darkness. I forsake all sin that may have given Satan a foothold in my life. I close all doors opened to his influence and separate my life from the fallen princi-palities and powers. I dedicate my life—body, soul, and spirit, to you. I place myself on your altar of service. I ask you, in Jesus' name, to remove from my life the lingering presence of evil and to fill me with your Spirit.

Resistance

Satan, I forsake you as a false god, a liar, a deceiver. I affirm Jesus as my Lord. I close the doors of your influence in my life, and overcome you with the blood of Jesus. I resist you and command you and your forces to leave me—go where Jesus Christ commands you to go.

For the Backslidden. I like to reason with backsliders. *Why* did you walk away from Jesus? *What* happened when you dropped out of Bible study? Most often there are specific issues, hurts, unanswered questions, broken relationships, disappointments in a church or a pastor, that provoke one's departure from faith. Engage these people in conversation. Dig out the questions, uncover the root feelings, then trust God for some answers. The Lord's answer for rebellious Israel was the pain of an oppressor, a breaking of will and pride through a circumstance out of one's control. Paul, remember, delivered Hymenaeus and Alexander over to Satan "to be taught not to blaspheme" (1 Tm 1:20). When normal means fail, drastic means sometimes become necessary. Let me share a prayer I have often used in this circumstance:

Prayer for Those Weakening in Their Faith

Lord, I bring _____ to you. Only you can know his or her heart. I cannot make _____ change—only you can. I pray you would open him or her up and help _____ to see what has made him or her walk away from you. Give me understanding to see those things as well. Holy Spirit, convict _____ of sin and stir up the desire to be right with you. Make _____ sick of sin. Do whatever you need to break his or her will, yet I ask you would be gentle. Bring an experience into _____'s life to encourage a return to you.

Father, in Jesus' name I subdue the influence of the enemy in _____'s life. I ask you to separate him or her from the lies and enticements of Satan. God, free _____ from this blindness. Shake him or her to his or her senses. Demonstrate the discipline of your love, yet do it in mercy. I praise and thank you for the work you are going to do in _____'s life.

THE PRAYER OF THE WATCHMAN

The Lord posted "watchmen" on the walls of Jerusalem, intercessors who would "never be silent," crying to God on behalf of the city and the people of Israel (Is 62:6). The Lord is stirring the hearts of many today to intercede for his church and for the work of world evangelism. I believe God is issuing a special calling for the labor of true intercession in this regard. But I also believe that every Christian is endowed with the authority of the Son, who himself has a perpetual ministry of intercession.

Increasingly, we should see ourselves as ambassadors of the invisible kingdom, watching for opportunities to act in faith. There are too many missed opportunities, dropped assignments. In any given day each of us has incredible potential to labor with Jesus for the needs of his church and the unsaved. We need to hold ourselves accountable for prayer that is endowed with a vision for kingdom expansion. Bold prayer emblazoned by faith and anointed with authority. Prayer that moves mountains.

The Lord is raising and posting watchmen on the walls of the new work he is doing in his church. A circle of intercession is being built in anticipation of the outpouring of his power in revival and harvest. We have an opportunity to enter into the battle of the kingdom work. Dick Eastman, author of *Love on Its Knees*, states that "prayer isn't so much another weapon on our list of weaponry as it is the actual battle itself."[1] If more lay people realized the power released in prayer, and began to practice it, the hand of God would move. Lord, give us more watchmen on the walls.

TEN

Strategies for the Struggle against Evil

*Prayer is man giving God a footing on the contested
territory of this earth. The man in full touch of purpose
with God, praying, insistently praying—that man is
God's footing on the enemy's soil. The man wholly
given over to God gives him a new sub-headquarters on
the battlefield from which to work out. And the Holy
Spirit within that man, on the new spot, will insist on
the enemy's retreat in Jesus the Victor's name. That is
prayer. Shall we not, every one of us, increase God's
footing down upon his prodigal earth?*

—S.D. Gordon

ONE RAINY AFTERNOON, I AND SIX others slowly made our way
to the top of Montserrat, the peak overlooking the city of
Bogota, Columbia. At the summit, we entered a Catholic
church and began to praise the Lord and to intercede for
the city below. We poured out our hearts: "Lord,
strengthen your servants in this land, send revival to your
people, break the strongholds of evil, bring a harvest of
souls."

One year later dramatic activity with Columbian drug smugglers was making headline news. Violence increased. But pastors and missionaries reported a powerful movement of the Holy Spirit at work in their churches and a new openness to the gospel.

I do not believe that our prayers alone turned the spiritual tide. But I do believe they added to the weight of intercession already invested and invading the enemy's territory.

I recall another time when several of us drove up to Mary's Peak, a location near my home, known for its witchcraft rituals. From that vantage point, we proclaimed God's praises to the heavens and out onto the Willamette Valley. We asked him to strengthen his people. This kind of intercessory prayer is a strategic *investment* that leads to an *increase* of the life of Christ within his body, a greater *intensity* of spiritual warfare, and, ultimately, the possibility of *divine intervention* in revival.

SPIRITUAL AUTHORITY: HOW FAR CAN WE GO?

Let me build a case for engaging in strategic warfare. Scripture is clear that Jesus delegated authority to his disciples, to act as ambassadors, and to do the works of ministry he did (Lk 10:17-20; Jn 14:12). This included authority over "all the power of the enemy" (Lk 10:19), authority to act on matters of church discipline (Mt 18:15-20), authority to be ambassadors of reconciliation in evangelism and discipleship (Mt 28:19; 2 Cor 5:18-20), and authority in teaching the truth (Mt 18:20; Ti 2:15).

Spiritual authority is to be exercised in efforts to personally overcome evil, to walk in truth, and to help set others free from sin and Satan. Jesus' prayer left a heavy responsibility in the laps of those called to leadership: "As you sent me into the world, I have sent them into the world" (Jn 17:18). "God raised us up with Christ and seated us with him in the heavenly realms" (Eph 2:6). He pours out divine grace for the exercise of spiritual authority. But Ephesians 3:10 also indicates that God has chosen to reveal his redemptive plan "through the church ... to the rulers and authorities in the heavenly realms." The proclamation of the Lordship of Jesus Christ involves a demonstration of redemption to the principalities and powers. In some measure, therefore, as co-heirs and co-rulers, we assert the authority of our King over the fallen powers, and over the effects they exert on people.

In the early 1980s, the Hindu guru Baghwan Shree Rajneesh bought land in central Oregon and built a city for his disciples. Over five thousand devotees came to sit under his teaching, which was expressly anti-Christian. Local residents, politicians, and law enforcement personnel tried different means to get the group out of Oregon, all to no avail. In 1986, I participated in two prayer meetings with several other experienced intercessors who led out in strategic intercession, petitioning the Lord to weaken the grip of the spiritual force working behind the commune. At the conclusion of these sessions, we sensed that the removal of the Baghwan was imminent. In 1987, several of the commune's leadership were indicted on legal charges, and within weeks the guru was deported, leaving a few scattered followers. Without question, prevailing prayer scattered the enemies of Yahweh.

Believers should engage in aggressive efforts to widen the kingdom, to establish strongholds of righteousness, oases of God's presence in the midst of spiritual pollution. The biblical realist knows that as long as evil men and institutions remain, doors will be opened for the continued infiltration of supernatural evil. But, the biblical realist also knows there are campaigns to be waged and victories to be won. The role of the soldier of Christ is to infiltrate the world system, give witness to the superiority of the heavenly kingdom, and cooperate with the Spirit's work of writing names in the Book of Life. Where wider momentum is gained, it *is* possible to see government leaders and nations submit to the Lordship of Christ and exemplify a microcosmic model of the kingdom. It is appropriate to pursue the fullest extent of God's plan for the transformation of society, being mindful that the kingdom cannot fully come until he returns in power.

I suggest that Christians aggressively claim and take individual lives, towns, institutions, territories, and nations for the glory of our Lord, always keeping in view the harvest and discipling of souls. Our God is in the business of proclaiming good news, binding up the brokenhearted, setting captives free, and planting oaks of righteousness, "for the display of his splendor" (Is 61:1-3). This, by his power, we are called to do.

BIBLICAL PRECEDENTS

A clear biblical mandate exists for exposing falsehood and false teachers, for setting people free from oppression, and for overcoming evil with good. But are we justified in escalating the conflict to the cosmic level? Are we treading on turf assigned to the angels? I think we *can* explore an appropriate approach for engaging in strategic warfare. Let's have a brief look first at some biblical models.

Moses, Elijah, and Daniel are three men who stood against the powers of their day. The strength of their faith brought down kings and kingdoms. Yet these men, models of intercession, were characterized by three things: each one was *sent* by God, *submitted* to the will of

God, and *sustained* by the power of prayer that focused on the sufficiency of God himself. When we look at each cosmic encounter, we should see men and women appointed and anointed by God for the task. I believe the Lord is calling us today to similar battles, but in the context of the corporate solidarity of the church and with the full exercise of spiritual gifts. If it is clear that we are sent into strategic battle, we can be sure God's power will prevail to sustain us and bring victory.

PRINCIPLES AND PERSPECTIVES

In line with Jesus' word to his disciples (Lk 10:17-20), *we must remember that the primary purpose of kingdom work is the writing of names in the book of life.* Power encounters must not become a preoccupation. We do not want to fall prey to the danger of embarking on a holy crusade to rid the world of evil. If our vision of God aching for the lost is blurred by a commando operation against the gates of hell, we miss the point.

We must *allow Jesus Christ to stage and wage our spiritual battles.* Pride and fascination with power can be dangerous temptations. Ask God to expose and check any fanaticism that flows from fleshly zeal. At this level of encounter, we must never presume ourselves to be God's chosen vessels.

This ministry is not for the untested. The one called to warfare should have experienced the sanctifying grace of the Spirit in areas of besetting sin (lust, anger, pride, deceit, ambition). Further, he or she should have undergone emotional healing that seals cracks of vulnerability (fear, false guilt, depression), and must know the empowerment of the Spirit for service. Such men and women should be mature, stable, submitted, and selflessly committed at any cost (1 Jn 2:12-14). Casualties will be minimized by culling out eager novices or those whose motivation is tainted.

Two distinct dimensions to power encounter must be understood as separate, yet related functions. The first is Godward—a sensitive abiding in and listening to the Holy Spirit, a receiving of clear impression and direction. Living a life of prayer is enhanced by the regular practice of praise (Eph 5:19, 20) and the outbreathing of petition and the inbreathing of peace and empowerment (Phil 4:6, 7).

The second dimension is a resistance against Satan, rooted in authority activated by prayer and empowered by truth. Unity of heart among participants is vital; they should be committed to one another as well as to the cause (Acts 1:14; 4:32). When seeking God's mind, they must ask in Jesus' name and ask according to his will and purpose (Mt 18:18-20; Acts 4:30). Their faith level is to be visionary and unwavering (Mk 11:22-25). And they must realize that their strategic stand will be tested.

An approach to power encounter that "takes on" the principalities with a view to staging a knockout punch to drive them out of a territory should be discouraged. Rather, it is my view that a proper interpretation of "struggling" against evil (Eph 6:12) and "overpowering" it (Lk 11:22) means entrance into a deeper, prolonged form of prayer, a laying hold of God that pleases him and prompts him to act. This kind of prayer involves a commitment to unity with fellow believers, and a commitment to bold incarnational truth, living those values of the kingdom that weaken and render evil ineffective. Something dynamic and eternal occurs in the heavenly realm when truth is lived. Often it is not immediately apparent or measurable. God's measure is character distilled through trial. Such character demonstrates the superiority of the way of Jesus and puts evil in its place.

TOWARD A WORKING MODEL FOR KINGDOM ADVANCEMENT THROUGH POWER ENCOUNTERS

This model is an approach for doing spiritual warfare within the context of Jesus' commission to win, teach, and disciple the lost (Mt 28:18-20). It may be used by a local church, a group of local believers, a mission organization, or any group of Christians called together with a common cause. It is set forth as a phased approach, covering an experimental span of three years. The length of time, however, depends on such variables as intensity of the resistance, spiritual health of the local church, and the level of faith. Elements of the model are flexible and must be adapted in terms of time and function to each context. Remember, this is simply a framework, a place to begin.

PHASE I: PREPARATION FOR BATTLE (SIX MONTHS)

Form a Core Community with Common Vision and Purpose. If God is at the center of your desire to enter spiritual warfare, he will begin to plant faith and prompt vision in the hearts of individuals throughout a community, on a mission field, or within an organization. The vision may emerge through the reading of Scripture, prompting in prayer, discouragement in the face of resistance, or the reading of materials on the topic of power encounter. A core group of at least four persons should begin to establish a commitment and accountability to seek God for instruction. The binding element should be: "Lord, show us your plan for bringing your kingdom into greater manifestation in this place."

I encourage this group to minister to one another through Scripture, prayer, and praise. Appropriate, by faith, the provision of the Lord's armor, through the blood of Jesus, the power of the Word, the shielding of the Spirit, and the ministry of the holy angels. Begin to engage in warfare against any personal harassment or attack which may begin or intensify.

Members of this group should maintain their customary ministries, such as pastoring, teaching, evangelizing, discipling, counseling, and so on. The group may be a loose, working network of individuals and may not take formal, organizational shape. Keep in mind that spiritual warfare takes the posture of authority that infuses ministry with the power of the Spirit which, in turn, increases the effectiveness of existing ministries.

Develop Resources, Conduct Good Research. The group should begin and sustain a study of the best materials available on the subjects of authority, discernment, gifts of the Spirit, deliverance procedures, and intercessory prayer. Set apart time to review the materials and to allow the Spirit to lead you to consensus on what rings true— keep the wheat, toss the chaff. Develop biblical, theological, and stylistic guidelines that fit your group.

Begin research into the ideologies, religious practices, and cultural sins that may invite and perpetuate demonic bondage in your locality. Cities or territories may have distinctive spiritual atmospheres. Research will bring to light the original conditions upon which a nation or city was established. Ask if these people or this place is characterized by greed, violence, immorality, incest, occultism, crime, or other sins. For example, at a Presbyterian Bible College in Hsinchu, Taiwan, students were experiencing disturbing visitations of spirits at night. It was later discovered the college was built on a Buddhist burial ground.

Begin Active Intercession. The key to doing battle is entering into identification with Christ in our intercession. This involves a willingness to partake of the sacrificial sufferings of Jesus and to prevail in faith-filled prayer that moves the hands of God. The intercessor holds the Word up before his throne and says boldly, "Lord, you have spoken this ... here is your promise ... act according to your Word." We cannot manipulate the Master. But he loves and responds to holy boldness.

The greater triumph will come not by targeting and railing against evil powers, but by strengthening the church. In united, prevailing prayer, move in the principles of Matthew 18:18-20 and Mark 11:22-25, and ask God to release his Spirit in the following directions:

- To strengthen, protect, heal, bless, and empower his leaders and key servants in this locality (Eph 6:18).

- To bring conviction of sin, righteousness, and judgment (Jn 16:8-11).

- To weaken the influence of evil spirits among unbelievers: to subdue their power, silence their voices, and separate their influence away from people, allowing for response to truth (Acts 26:17, 18).

- To work according to Acts 4:29, 30: asking God to enable his servants to proclaim the Word with boldness, and to stretch out his hand to perform miracles in the name of Jesus.

Seek the Lord for Revelation of Strongholds. Learn to ask questions and listen for the Lord's answers. What persons, institutions, ideologies, or cultural sins are the channels through which the principalities operate to promote deception and bondage in this location? Who or what governs the anti-Christian agenda here? Based on what I see in the lives of people, and what I sense intuitively, what are the spiritual powers that shape and dominate their attitudes and actions? What is it like to live in this place? What spiritual hassles and pressures do people experience here?

PHASE II: THE SHAPING OF STRATEGY (ONE YEAR)

Continue Building Up the Church. If your efforts succeed in putting pressure on the powers of darkness, you may experience some kickback. The early church learned this, as they "devoted themselves to the apostles' teaching, and to the fellowship, to the breaking of bread and to prayer" (Acts 2:42). Opposition to the expansion of the church arose from within and without. Keep current with personal needs and struggles. Troubleshoot and deal with any oppression. Regularly allow for sharing and prayer. Remember, building up and unifying the body in love will ultimately do the devil the most damage.

Gather Data from Research and Ministry. Ask, "What is God showing us?" Draw some preliminary conclusions from deliverance sessions, observed patterns of bondage, and research. Identify individuals, organizations, and cultural practices that seem to be the focus of negative power. Try to name the force that may work behind and through these mediums. Match these observations with impressions gained from prayer and from interviews with church and ministry leaders. Ponder the data for a while. Ask, and wait for the Spirit to confirm or discount the information. Enter into constant prayer and come together as a group to sharpen the interpretation of the data.

Implement Selected Strategies. I believe that many appropriate actions can be taken during this strategizing phase. With good leadership and clarity in prayer, transition to mobilization may occur in a short span of time. Here are several active strategies to begin your response to the data.

- *Regular Intercession:* Some people will be called to closet prayer, the behind the scenes prevailing with God and wrestling with the devil that releases real power for outward ministry. Individual and group intercession must be encouraged and sustained. Many communities now have quarterly "Concerts of Prayer" open to all churches. These can have a significant and lasting spiritual impact.

- *Faith Walks:* In view of Abraham's charge to "walk about the land" and claim it, and Joshua's instruction to encircle Jericho, the Lord may direct groups to walk through a city and claim it for God. Expect the Spirit to sharpen your discernment, stir faith, and prompt you in prayer and praise to loose his power to penetrate darkness. This is a long-term, visionary endeavor. Praise marches or rallies that verbally and visibly proclaim the Lordship of Jesus may have a profound impact on both the people *in* the community and the powers *over* the community.

- *Doing Deeds of Justice:* God honors and blesses deeds of caring for the poor, tending to the needs of the helpless and fatherless, and helping the oppressed. Involvement in prison ministries, inner city work, orphanages, anti-abortion efforts, drug and alcohol rehabilitation are all means whereby evil is exposed and weakened. The practice of incarnational love that validates Jesus and liberates people from Satan's lies and bondage must be a centerpiece of spiritual warfare. No magical substitute exists for the sacrificial obedience of doing the will of God.

- *Evangelism:* In the fresh light of spiritual warfare, we must allow the Spirit to teach us how to cooperate with him in binding spiritual forces that block penetration of the gospel. We must become more accustomed to exercising authority in order to silence, subdue, and separate satanic influence from the one being drawn by the Spirit to respond to Christ. In leading people to salvation, we should be more thorough in leading persons to forsake areas of satanic advantage, allowing for more immediate practical freedom in addition to positional freedom from the enemy.

- *Establish Deliverance Ministries:* Ideally, at least one person or team working in discernment and deliverance should be available in the community. It is not realistic to expect this of every local church. Such ministries need not be conducted within a local body, but those involved must work under the authority of a local fellowship.

Begin Apprenticeship Training. At some point during this phase, start training a hands-on approach to developing spiritual skills. My approach is to have others follow me around, watch what I do and when I do it, and pick up what the Lord gives them. We need environments where folks learn by doing what they see others do. Those wanting to learn the practice of intercession should attend meetings devoted to that purpose and simply watch and absorb. Those called to deliverance should look for a pastor or mature spiritual advisor who has had exposure sufficient enough to provide knowledge and training.

PHASE III: MOBILIZATION (ONE YEAR)

Maintain and Fine-Tune the Practice of Body Life. The core team should continue to meet regularly for dialogue, sharing in the Word and prayer, and ministry to one another. In light of Paul's exhortation to "be alert and always keep on praying for all the saints" (Eph 6:18), we must troubleshoot personal struggles and spiritual attacks that arise. Discouragement, disillusionment, and confusion can burden a team. Watch for obvious harassment of a person or family and for the more subtle assaults on areas of emotional weakness and besetting sin. The quicker these strategies are detected, the easier they are to deal with. Watch for these symptomatic indicators of oppression: uncontrolled fear, extreme discouragement, a wedge of anger or mistrust between team members, undiagnosed ailments, inability to get clear leading from the Lord, and excessive temptation.

Guard against attitudinal sins of pride, jealousy, criticism, and resentment. Maintain the perspective of God's overarching sovereignty. Inject a sufficient amount of laughter and lightness in the midst of battle. It's therapeutic to take ourselves and the burden of battle less seriously, and it helps to sustain the morale of the group.

Continue Apprenticeship Training. By this stage, four major groups should be active: the leadership core group that provides vision and overall leadership; an intercessory prayer team; deliverance teams; and various functional ministry teams (street witnessing, youth ministry, crisis counseling, written communications, and so on). Those comfortable with and confident in spiritual warfare will bring others into an apprenticeship relationship to model the lifestyle of authority, reliance on the Spirit, and demonstration of the gifts.

Intensify Intercession. Gradually, the quality and quantity of prevailing prayer should increase. Continue the positive focus of petitioning the Lord to pour out his Spirit on his servants, the churches, and the community. Pray

Acts 4:29 with holy boldness. It is also appropriate to target and tear down strongholds that have been identified. It may be a particular person (political figure, New Age leader, a witch), an institution (local government, religious body, social service organization, a cult), or a demonic stronghold over your area (sexual perversion, witchcraft, greed). Here is a pattern for prayer that may be helpful:

- *The Principle:* Apply Christ's authority to expand kingdom horizons, believing and asking God to work through his Spirit and the angelic hosts to penetrate and push back the evil powers, thus enhancing the growth of the church and the work of the harvest.

- *The Petition:* Prayer at this level is visionary, bold, and prevailing. Pattern Prayer: "Lord, you are the Almighty—we affirm your sovereign dominion over _____. By faith, we write the triumphant name of Jesus above this city and claim it for your glory. The scepter of the wicked will not remain over the land you have given to your people (Ps 125:1, 2). The battle is not ours, but yours (2 Chr 20:15). We ask you to penetrate and weaken the stronghold of religious deception over this area. Commission your holy angels to do battle with the principalities. Thank you for scattering the enemy. We praise you for your faithfulness."

- *The Prompting to Act:* Follow the lead of the Spirit to do any "on sight" prayer, *e.g.*, praying outside an abortion clinic, pornography shop, or New Age bookstore. The Lord is the one in charge. *Let him lead you in his plan for your community.*

PHASE IV: EVALUATION AND REPLICATION

Evaluation. Because these activities are focused on the supernatural, measurement of success is not always obvious. It is dangerous to rely on subjective impressions to answer the question, "How are we doing?" There must be objective criteria by which we determine movement in the right direction. Ask the hard questions. Has our discernment been correct? Are we slipping into any doctrinal error? Have there been casualties? Does any person involved need correction or exhortation?

It is necessary also to measure the effectiveness of your efforts. Has there been a noticeable increase of unity of heart and common purpose among the believers and churches? Is there a balanced deliverance team functioning? Are there visible signs of strongholds weakening? Are there signs of fresh, measurable growth among the churches? Can we honestly say that the kingdom is advancing in this place?

If evaluation and measurement are positive, God may open doors to multiply the success. Be open to his leading to share with other individuals, organizations, and communities what has happened in your locality. To give your experience substance, it helps to document in writing what you have developed. This can serve as a model or pattern which can be adapted to other situations in other locales. Trust the Lord to anoint those on the team gifted in teaching and preaching to record the model for kingdom advancement you have learned.

KEEPING A RIGHT PERSPECTIVE

Let's understand that we will not be completely rid of evil until God deals a death blow to Satan. Let's be realistic and acknowledge that cities and countries that have seen profound revival have, several generations later, slipped back into ungodliness. No permanent geographical expression of the kingdom will exist short of the coming King. But we must model our identity as "more than conquerors" and demonstrate that the gates of hell will not prevail against the people of God.

Recently I traveled to Taiwan to train pastors in deliverance and intercession. One evening, we identified a major deity of materialism recognized throughout Taiwan. After a time of praise and worship, the group listened for the Lord, in silence. Then, one by one we petitioned him to penetrate and weaken the grip of greed in the land.

A strange thing then occurred. After we had been praying for about fifteen minutes, I noticed that several pastors were getting involved in intense personal dialogue, diverting the direction of the prayer time. I asked my translator what was going on. He was drawn into the intensity himself. Then he told me there were both mainland and Taiwanese Chinese present, and strong feelings of hurt and hatred were surfacing that traced back to the struggle for Taiwan's independence. Resentment, hatred, and mistrust were being confessed to one another. The honest, painful exchange went on for several hours. There were tears of forgiveness and reconciliation. The Spirit was tending to priorities, mending the broken body. As I reflected on the evening, the real meaning of Ephesians 3:1-13 came to light. Here was the true victory, the miracle of reconciliation. This is what is to be "made known to the principalities and powers," and to the watching world—the supremacy of love that demonstrates the goodness and glory of God. If we could but love one another with the same intensity and fervor with which we tackle problems and projects, there would be more damage done to evil than all of our zealous agendas could achieve.

May the strategic discernment and penetration of strongholds *not* become another fanatical agenda or misplaced priority. May it be an endeavor entrusted to healthy groups of Christians whose priorities are right, and who are ready to pay the price of prevailing in the power of the Most High God to participate in strategic advances of his kingdom.

ELEVEN

What Everyone Seems to Want to Know about Spiritual Warfare

God has given us in his Book sufficient knowledge regarding the devil to help us, both as to our attitude toward the enemy and as to the weapons that we are to use in conflict with him.

But biblical students as a rule are indifferent to the subject. It is not popular nor agreeable; yet God holds us responsible for this ignorance of what he has revealed to us regarding Satan. . . . Satan thrives on this ignorance. . . . The light of truth is his undoing; expose the foe by the light of truth. Challenge him by the victory of the Cross and he is defeated. He is a broken power.

—Charles Usher

AFTER PRACTICING SPIRITUAL WARFARE for twenty years, I have heard most of the questions that come up on this topic. I've sifted through hundreds of questions that have issued from seminars, letters, consultations, and conversations, and I think it would help to take a crack at some of the "head scratchers." Most of these are not theoretical, but practical questions. Short of direct revelation, some measure of speculation will always be mixed with the answers. But certain principles and patterns have emerged from many years of experience. I offer them here in the hope that they may help those who find themselves engaged in warfare.

Can Satan, or evil spirits, read your thoughts? This question comes up frequently. I think not. Most others agree with me. If a Christian is free from internal demonization, the enemy cannot read his or her thoughts from the inside out. I believe that "minds set on what the Spirit desires" (Rom 8:5) are a sanctuary impenetrable by unholy spirits. This has been proven to me in deliverance sessions, where demons do not know the strategy for expelling them that I am weighing in my mind. And yet, let's recognize that these beings have been in the business of deceiving and afflicting people since the creation of man and are adept at predicting behavior. By reading facial expressions, voice intonations, and behavioral nuances, they can often predict what we are going to do. But this does not mean they have access to our innermost thoughts. However, within the demonized believer, spirits have more ready access to thoughts.

Evil beings may indeed project thoughts into the mind, moods into the emotions, and impulses into the will from their external vantage point. This is the stuff of which most spiritual warfare is made. But the battle must be characterized primarily as from the outside in, rather than the inside out.

How can I tell the difference between the voice of the Holy Spirit and evil spirits? God will never speak anything that is contrary to his revealed Word or character. I have found that the Holy Spirit is gentle, clear, and consistent in his leading. He leads by an inward prompting that has a "ring of rightness" to it. Often other persons or circumstances will confirm his voice. If we are truly submitted to him, we will be open to the scrutiny and correction of others. The voice of God will always result in redemptive purpose. Fruit will flow from the promptings of the Father.

The devil, on the other hand, is sly, often bringing doubts and questions concerning the reliability of God's character. An evil spirit compels a certain thought or behavior, and leaves us in a state of confusion and heaviness. The enemy seeks always to lead us into isolation from other believers, groping and grappling with our thoughts and feelings. Devilish promptings lead to unfruitful dead ends. Often, only time can fully tell whether we have followed the voice of the Spirit, the voice of the enemy, or our own carnal thoughts. Our protection is to abide in the Word and to remain accountable to godly leadership in a local church.

How can I discern between a human impulse and demonic temptation? This question is similar to the previous one, and very important. How can I know where my human impulses leave off and the influence of a spirit begins? In my counseling practice, I encounter many people who wrestle with such problems as anger, lust, and overeating. They are overtaken by some *thing*, an *it* of sorts that compels behavior. But let's not be too quick to call this demonic. In Romans 7, Paul describes sin in strong terms as a sort of foreign force, an *it* that compels me to do what my spiritual man doesn't want and hinders me from doing what I *do* want. Ruts of mind and grooves of the will are strong, deep, and seem to have a life of their own.

James described carnality as "earthly, unspiritual, of the devil" (Jas 3:15). This covers the bases. In a sense, such struggles do overlap with the world, the flesh, and the devil. It is hard, and often pointless, to try to nail down the exact source. Our response should be the same: be ready to repent of sin, reject false values of the world, and resist Satan as enticer. Generally, it is wise to assume our struggle to be of the flesh, that which we can do something about. Here is a practical approach to answer the question: confess it as sin, reckon yourself dead to it, and receive the Lord's forgiveness. Peace and increased control of the Holy Spirit should follow, even if you repeat the process. If there is no peace or victory through treating this as carnality, you would be wise to pray with a discerning Christian to check for oppression.

What are the typical ways in which people come to be oppressed? Spiritual oppression is not a haphazard occurrence. There *are* principles that govern the warfare. Through numerous encounters with oppressed individuals, I have identified four major sources of oppression: 1. Through the personal, persistent practice of moral compromise (either as unbeliever or believer) that opens doors to the influence of evil spirits. This seems to occur primarily in sins of the occult (any form of idolatry); the reactive sins of anger, bitterness, and hate; persistent sexual sin, or fleshly indulgence; 2. Through the sins of others in one's family history that have opened doors to evil spirits which then try to influence and invade "downline" generations; 3. Through the victimizing sins of others, *e.g.*, rape, incest, violent acts, exposure to occultic ritual; 4. Through ministry activity that draws attention from the enemy.

In the first three occurrences, there is usually ignorance and nonrecognition of Satan's schemes altogether. As Christians, however, we should learn to be equipped to discern and deal with oppressive influence. Deliverance from all evil is one of the major ministries of the Lord Jesus to the redeemed person.

In resistance, must my prayers be audible or can I pray silently? Based on the models of Jesus and Paul, audible rebuke of the enemy seems to be most effective. Remember, the "sword of the Spirit" is the *rhema*, the spoken word. Demons by nature try to defy truth. A clear, authoritative word is necessary to drive them out, or away. When it is appropriate to speak, use the Scriptures, speak in faith, and believe the Spirit is with you to back up the word.

There will be times, however, when you cannot offer audible prayer or rebuke. Great pressure is put upon spirits with concerted prayer that is silent and focused. Bear down on the enemy with the eye of discernment and let him know that you know who's in charge. Assert Jesus' authority and supremacy. This kind of prayer can occur in the midst of conversation or normal activities. It is especially effective in praying with family members, in church services when demons seem to be disrupting things, in public settings, and in the midst of ministry when you discern the enemy is hindering your effectiveness. Prayer, to be effective, does not necessarily need to be verbalized.

What problems are often incorrectly thought to be demonic? After many years of exposure to a broad spectrum of problems, I have found a number of demonic "look-alikes." We must be careful not to quickly attribute certain strange symptoms to evil spirits. I always ask this question: "Is there present an identifiable, alien force of evil separate from this personality that responds negatively to the authority of Christ and the presence of his Spirit?" Just as we see in Scripture, we should see manifestation of a distinct entity that is observably opposed to the person of Jesus Christ.

Let me categorize a few common problems that may look like, but most often are not demonic: 1. *Physical* (organic or biochemical causation): hormonal imbalances (premenstrual syndrome, postpartum psychosis), certain anxiety reactions, allergies, epilepsy, Alzheimer's, schizophrenia, clinical depression, manic depression; 2. *Emotional:* severe emotional damage or deprivation, circumstantial depression, fear, extreme low self-esteem; 3. *Psychological:* phobias (such as fear of heights, crowds, small rooms), obsessive-compulsive disorders, character disorders; 4. *Behavioral:* compulsive disorders and addictions (eating, gambling, drugs, pornography).

It is often difficult to know for sure what the real source of the problem is. Some of the above may be caused by evil spirits. An inherent human problem may be aggravated by spirits. Professionals involved in the various healing disciplines should be working with pastors and others in the deliverance ministry. Expertise in spiritual sight and wisdom should complement expertise in the medical and psychological realms.

How can you distinguish between a psychiatric disorder and demonization? I have prayed with a number of people suffering from schizophrenia, manic depression, multiple personality disorder, and psychotic episodes. In some cases, demons attach to and aggravate the condition. In others, there is clear psychiatric malfunction. With such disorders, there are such symptoms as internal voices, extreme paranoia, religious delusions, and uncontrolled behaviors. Dr. Kurt Koch, psychiatrist and author of *Occult Bondage and Deliverance*, made the valuable observation that the mentally ill person is quick to talk about voices and spirits, whereas the truly demonized individual is typically not—evil spirits want to stay hidden.

I have learned to distinguish these disorders from demonization through careful observation (these disorders fit predictable patterns with observable symptoms), and through testing at two levels. First, I seek to interact with a person over certain truths concerning Jesus Christ or the Word of God. I may ask him to read a portion of Scripture. Often, I will open an interview with prayer. I watch for clear negative reaction to authority and the working of the Holy Spirit. On a second level, if the person is agreeable, I will do a direct test: with eyes open, relying on the Holy Spirit, I will command any enemies of Christ present to manifest and make themselves known. Still, it is important to realize that a mentally disturbed person can easily "create" a demon if you ask for one. Proven, accurate discernment is necessary to distinguish a demon from a disorder.

Can spirits be cast out of a person at a distance? Occasionally, yes, but only with the moral and spiritual cooperation of the person. Deliverance must not be attempted on one unwilling to submit to God, deal with sin, and make a commitment to Christ (Jas 4:6-10). For demons to remain "gone," the house must be cleaned and filled with the Spirit of Christ. To confront spirits in a person not ready to submit to God is to "stir up the hornets": it may make matters worse.

For those in need of deliverance, I advise a two-track mode of binding and loosing prayer. I ask the Spirit to make the person sick of his or her sin, to plant seeds of truth in the mind, and, if for an unbeliever, to stir the person to seek salvation. I also ask the Spirit to actively silence, subdue, and separate demonic influence from the person, thus allowing him or her to respond to truth.

Having done this, I wait and watch for God to open doors and bring opportunity to work directly with the one in bondage.

Can you cast spirits out of children? Most children I have prayed for have come under spiritual bondage through one of four avenues: 1. pagan parents; 2. familial spirits that have come down through the ancestry; 3. pagan parents that have given a child up for adoption; 4. victimization, the "rub off" effect of physical or sexual abuse, exposure to the occult, and severe traumas that open doors to demonic influence.

Generally, at the request of a parent or guardian, we may pray for children up to about the age of nine or ten, when personal moral accountability necessitates their own decision (accountability must be discerned on an individual basis). I have found the Lord merciful and quick to deliver afflicted children. With the parent holding or touching a child, I move in authority to remove the ground of oppression with the blood of Jesus and the sword of the Spirit, commend the child to God's care, and command the evil spirits to leave quickly and permanently. Expulsion is often quick, dramatic, and immediately observable. Believing parents may also pray for natural or adopted children at home, either holding them while awake, or laying a hand on them while asleep.

Symptoms of oppression in children include violent, malicious behavior, cursing, sexual acting out, extreme fear, facial contortions, and rebellion against parents and authority figures.

Recent books on spiritual warfare suggest that prayer enables angels to accomplish God's will. Is this notion biblical? Scripture is clear that angels are commissioned by God as agents for the outworking of his will: to bring messages, to administer judgment, and to minister grace and protection to the redeemed. There is ample Old Testament evidence that prayer and obedience please God and in some way release his power to overcome enemies.

Second Kings 6 records Elisha's prayer that opened the eyes of his servant to see the invisible warriors sent to defeat the forces of the king of Aram. David calls to the Lord and is saved out of his troubles. In connection to the calling, "the angel of the LORD" comes to the aid of the servant of God (Ps 34:6, 7). Trusting and calling on God is also described in Psalm 91, where God also is said to "command his angels" to deliver the saint in trouble. Shadrach, Meshach, and Abednego were joined in the king's furnace by an angel. Telling Nebuchadnezzar of his escape from the lions, Daniel says, "My God sent his angel" (6:22). And after Daniel's twenty-one-day fast, Gabriel appeared and indicated that his praying was connected with his and Michael's battle with satanic "princes" (Dn 10:13-20).

The connection between prayer and angelic operation did not cease in the early church. With Peter in prison (Acts 12), the church prayed earnestly, and an angel came to set the Apostle free. Acts 12:15 gives evidence of the possibility of personal guardian angels. There *is* a connection between the calling and the outworking of God's will. But we cannot know, nor should we try to find out, the extent to which the angels are dependent upon our prayers. That is God's business, and he hasn't given us a lot of light on it. Our proper responsibility is to earnestly pray and trust God to work. Our confidence must be that when we pray in faith, the Lord hears and chooses the means through which he will work.

Are there specific days or seasons when evil forces are stronger? Yes, there are definite times when practitioners of occultism, witchcraft, and satanism engage in certain rituals. These times often coincide with astronomical changes, such as new and full moons, the summer and winter solstices, and the fall and spring equinoxes. Such observances trace back to ancient pagan practices related to the worship of astral deities.

There are documented unholy days when certain rituals and sacrifices (animal and human) are performed in formal satanism: February 2, March 20 (Spring Equinox), April 26-May 1, June 21 (Summer Solstice), August 3, September 22 (Fall Equinox), October 29-November 1 (All Hallow's Eve), and December 22-24 (Winter Solstice). Christians should be aware that hideous abuse of children, defamation of Christ, and human sacrifices do occur on these dates. We should follow the Lord's signals in prayer. Some of us can sense or feel the added presence and power of evil in the atmosphere on certain days or seasons. The enemy is more active during these times, and thus appears to be stronger than at other times.

How should we respond during these times? We should watch for an increase in depression, discouragement, and disturbance of sleep. We should abide in prayer, guarding ourselves, family members, and fellow workers. We must learn to pray with knowledge and discernment, releasing the light of the Holy Spirit to penetrate and weaken the effects of darkness, and to convict those practicing these things and lead them to truth. These dates and seasons should be opportunities for the church to enter into strong praise, worship, and celebration of the Lordship of Christ.

How can I discern the difference between a normal dream and a demonic disturbance? This is a common question. We must understand that dreams have a strange nature all their own. They are prompted by a combination of conscious reality with unconscious fears and desires, and they comprise a mixing of symbol and imagery. Often, normal dreams involve sexual content and violence (either fear of harm, or causing harm to others). It seems true enough that things both desired and dreaded find expression in the dream state. These manifestations should not bother us. Negative effects of normal dreams seem to clear up within hours after awakening.

You can suspect demonic activity when one or more of the following factors seems true: 1. you awaken in a state of extreme terror or heaviness that does not clear up shortly after you awaken; 2. A distinct evil presence is perceived in the waking state following the dream; 3. you feel separated from God's peace—confused and fearful; 4. there are distinct satanic symbols, faces, or verbal threats; 5. the negative symptoms do not clear up when you or your spouse or a friend prays. A distinct demonic attack may be characterized by both evil presence and physical paralysis—inability to move or speak.

Christian workers involved in strategic ministry report increased night harassment. If possible, pray aloud, reciting Scripture. Apply the power of Jesus' blood to cover your mind, and command anything sent to harass you to leave immediately. If night visitations continue, there is likely to be a reason for it—seek out someone gifted in discernment and deliverance.

If I am walking in obedience to the Lord, is there any danger of being harassed by an evil spirit? I treat this question at length elsewhere in the book, but it is important to address again. I want to dismiss needless paranoia. We can see from the account of Job that there are rules to the adversary's game of accusing and afflicting people. God does not allow haphazard spiritual oppression. If demons are drawn to a person, it is traceable to sin in one's ancestry, personal sin before or after conversion, an experience of victimization or trauma, or direct encounter with someone involved in darkness.

The believer *is* responsible to understand the battle. We cannot plead ignorance. Paul encourages forgiveness of the Corinthian brother "in order that Satan might not outwit us. For we are not unaware of his schemes" (2 Cor 2:11). To be unaware is thus to be vulnerable. He also exhorts us strongly to "stand" against evil forces (Eph 6:10-18). To be naive or weak in facing warfare may leave openings. We must understand that there are agents of Satan who curse and send spirits against pastors, missionaries, and other workers. To take seriously the armor of God is to insure our shielding. Failure to deal with sin may leave us vulnerable to a satanic foothold (Eph 4:27). I believe the Spirit is clear in convicting us and leading us to repent. The power of our Lord to shield us from evil is fully available, if we simply walk in trust and according to the whole counsel of the Scriptures.

What can I do if I seem to be abnormally harassed by someone at work? These days, increasing numbers of people are involved in anything from trance channeling to witchcraft. If you end up on the bad side of someone in an employment situation, you face a difficult challenge. You cannot avoid the person. Neither can you bring up the true nature of your concern. If the person through whom demonic energy seems to extend is also a superior, the situation is more complex.

I suggest the following: 1. Don't assume too quickly that evil spirits are involved. Do your best to document occult involvement. This is difficult if there is no clear evidence, and the person is afflicted with ancestral demons; such people will often not know their own bondage. Ask: Is this a matter of personality, or is there another issue involved? 2. Do nothing to knowingly provoke the person to greater dislike. Without compromising yourself, work to avoid unnecessary conflict. 3. Pray. Seek and receive regularly the Lord's shielding, and actively speak blessing back to the person in prayer and also with direct kindness. Enlist the prayers of others, and send the Holy Spirit to subdue and contain the negative influence. 4. Be truly willing to endure hardship and the suffering of injustice; if either demons or a malicious person (or both) are involved, your Christian character is being assaulted by evil and tested by God. 5. Be spiritually assertive, establish your turf with a spiritual authority that is gentle but firm. 6. As clearly led, walk through open doors to dialogue with this person about spiritual things, then wait and watch God work.

What should I do if I know that my relatives or in-laws have been involved in the occult, *e.g.*, spiritualism, witchcraft, or cults? Even if you are currently a believer, it is possible that familial spirits may still be assigned to you. You will want to "build a spiritual dam" between you and the downstream flow of unconfessed sin that has allowed for demonic accusation. Work through a prayer of renunciation as outlined in Chapter Four, and separate yourself and your children from enemies of Christ that may have lingered.

You will want to prepare for personal contact with unsaved family members. Not only do these familial relationships stir up emotions related to the old life, but any evil spirits still present in relatives know your weaknesses and will try to attack them if your guard is down. This is one reason why holiday and vacation visits home are often so difficult. Be sure to spend time in the Scriptures before the contact, reestablishing your spiritual roots and identity. Be aware of your emotional and psychological weak areas. Cover yourself and children with spiritual protection, and enlist prayer support from friends. If you are staying in the home of a family member, make it a point to have a quiet time with the Lord once a day.

When interacting with family, offer silent, focused prayers to expose and weaken generational strongholds. Claim family members for salvation, ask God for open doors, and wait for him to work. Generally, our own zealous efforts to convince and convert family members are a dismal failure. Most often, our own faithfulness to live a testimony and pray secretly to God is most effective. The Lord often uses others to harvest the fruit after we have watered the seed through many years and tears.

If I suspect that someone is under demonic influence, what can I do to encourage the person to seek help? Always demonstrate Jesus' love, be available, and do not scare the person off by suggesting demonic bondage too early. If you are concerned about someone who is a Christian, you might suggest a book, such as Mark Bubeck's *The Adversary*, or Chuck Swindoll's pamphlet entitled *Demonism*. If people are desperate and ready to deal with their struggle, it is usually appropriate to ask whether they have considered whether their problem is related to oppression.

Remember, you cannot make moral responses for other people, regardless of how much you suffer for them. A sacred freedom of will is involved here. The Lord won't move in until there is a breaking of will and the opening of the door a crack. So it is appropriate to pray, "Lord, paint this person into a corner, and make him sick of his sin … let him see the seriousness of his bondage, and seek you for help."

What is the right response to a teenager who is into such things as heavy metal music, occult or sensual posters, rebellious attitudes, and questionable friends? Violent, destructive powers *are* targeting youth today. Alert Christians are actively battling for the safety and salvation of young people. Be patient and persevering in your prayer, asking especially on a regular basis for the protection of your child: "Jesus, place your hand on _____, shield him or her from the work of the evil one. Restrain him or her from decisions that will bring permanent harm. I apply the power of your blood to this life. Send your holy angels as a guard, and to lead _____ back to you. Hear my prayers—preserve and protect my son or daughter."

Establish values and standards at home. You will probably encounter a fight over music, dress, room decor, attitudes, and so on. Hold the line on standards, and trust God to guide you if and when you should be flexible. I would never allow certain posters or record albums into my home. When your children are away, spend time in their rooms inviting the Holy Spirit to fill the place and commanding evil spirits to leave.

Speak matter-of-factly about the dangers of demonic influence. Try not to use a moralizing, legalistic tone. Say what needs to be said, pray, and trust the Lord to work. Arrange for your children to be exposed to other healthy peer or adult role models. Surviving the crucible of the teen years is a trial for many. Keep the big picture of God's faithfulness in view, and keep showering your children with petitions to God for protection. Stand solidly on the assurances of Psalm 102:28 and 103:17, 18 regarding the children of the righteous. Ask God to honor your faith and work according to his Word. Be aware, however, that the foundation for a healthy spiritual life must be built from the early years up. When a teen gets into trouble, you may have to painfully admit that you did "too little too late" to model real Christianity. If this happens, entrust yourself and your problem child to the Lord's mercy, and hope and pray for the best outcome.

Is there any danger in watching television or movies with occultic or sensual content? The real danger here is that movies can conduct a visual and verbal assault on our senses that stirs carnality, misdirects the mind, and potentially opens doors of influence. At the risk of sounding like a fanatical crusader, I must say that many who produce the visual media are either devoid of godly values or dabbling in occult metaphysics, or both. Afternoon "soaps" to movies focusing on sex and violence, all contain themes and images that penetrate the mind and leave a believer vulnerable to demonic influence.

Years ago I let Psalm 101:3 be my guide: "I will set before my eyes no worthless things." Sin is not simply wrong behavior. It has its roots in the mind (see Jas 1:14, 15). Today, especially, we must decisively determine to set and keep to certain standards about what goes into our minds. I believe a strategy exists to stimulate children's interest in the occult through cartoons that feature sorcerers and fantasy figures who possess occultic power. We should be training our children about what shows not to watch and why. As parents, we cannot indulge in a double standard. We have to display a discerning selectivity in what *we* allow to enter our own senses.

What are the most important aspects of achieving victory in spiritual warfare? The first ingredient to victory is recognizing the possibility of warfare. Many of us are so slow to acknowledge the working of evil forces. If the devil can keep us in the dark with our weapons in the closet, we are defeated. Second, we must learn to call on God more quickly in prayer to ask for light on our circumstance and for deliverance if necessary. If this is a trial, it is ordained or allowed by God for a purpose. If a tribulation from Satan, it can and should be removed.

Third, the key to immediate victory is to use the weapons of the truth, the name and blood of Jesus, prayer and praise in an active, authoritative manner. Lay persons especially need to understand that they have authority to resist and repel evil. And fourth, a general perspective: learn better how the Holy Spirit guides you. He is the source of divine power within you and will enlighten you about how to respond in any situation.

TWELVE

Tips from the Trench: Words to the Wise

We constantly pray for you, that our God may count you worthy of his calling, and that by his power he may fulfill every good purpose of yours and every act prompted by your faith. We pray this so that the name of our Lord Jesus Christ may be glorified in you, and you in him, according to the grace of our God and the Lord Jesus Christ.   2 Thes 1:11, 12

"NO, LORD, I DON'T LIKE THAT IDEA... let someone else do it." The setting was a posh resort club in the Rocky Mountains. The scene was a symposium of psychologists, psychiatrists, theologians, and journalists. I had prepared a presentation on discernment and deliverance, but in the friendly skies somewhere over Wyoming another impression began brewing: God doesn't just want me to lecture—he has something more for me to do. With that thought came the idea that someone in this group needed spiritual help, and after my lecture I was to open the meeting for prayer. My audience was to be a diverse Christian group—an assortment of liberals, evangelicals, and charismatics. There probably would be considerable resistance to my suggestion.

"Who am *I*, Lord?" (I relate well to Moses, Gideon and Jeremiah!) "Trust me and obey," said the Spirit. I'm the non-imposing, diplomatic type. What right did Tom White have to pray for this bunch? I didn't sleep the night before the lecture.

After the lecture the next afternoon, I overcame my fears and obeyed the Lord: "I believe that someone here may relate personally to what I've presented and may need prayer." Some shook their heads affirmatively, eager to pray right away. Others were nervous. "Who is this guy, anyway? How do we know we can trust him?" We broke for dinner, and then regathered, only to find ourselves again divided over whether to let me start praying. Tension built within me: "Lord, what are you going to do? This is not fun."

Then a brother came from across the circle, knelt down, and whispered, "The Lord is with you, go ahead." Moments later, a psychotherapist from the East Coast suddenly took control of the group with an emotive appeal: "Let the man do his thing!" Little did anyone know—I had no *thing* in mind! I just began to pray, turned the meeting over to the Holy Spirit, and waited. Within minutes, the room filled with the holy presence of God. As we all sat in silence and awe, a woman got up and carried her chair to the center of the room: "I'm a victim of incest. . . . When Tom was speaking earlier, something very dark surfaced within me. . . . I feel such fear and hatred toward my father. I've got to deal with this."

What followed was wonderful. Gathering in a circle of prayer around this woman, we exposed three afflicting spirits that had taken advantage of her victimization, and led her through complete deliverance. The evening went on. Another attendee, an unbeliever, watched as we worked with the other woman. The Spirit moved on her, and she opened her heart to receive Christ. Others requested prayer. A fountain of healing love flowed into that room.

How vitally important it is to learn the secret of listening for and following the signals of the Spirit. If we obey his promptings and wait for him to act, he will break into our midst. Sometimes obedience feels very risky and uncomfortable, as it was in my situation. However, the reward of obedience and trust is great—it is worth our leap of faith.

RELATIONSHIPS: THE KEY CONTEXT OF SPIRITUAL WARFARE

Anyone who gets involved in spiritual warfare quickly learns that the struggle with evil does not occur in a mystical, ethereal vacuum. It always connects in some way to human relationships. Jesus' priestly prayer for our protection from the evil one calls us to love and unity as the body of Christ on earth. Our protection and strength against evil depends upon our practice of love.

Edgardo Silvoso, the director of Harvest Evangelism in San Jose, related the story of revival in his native land of Argentina. Several men fasted and prayed, asking God to break the power of the ruling spirits over certain cities. The results were remarkable. Ed said church leaders came to ask him how they could get involved in this warfare. He gave them wise counsel: "Get the elders or deacons in your church to work at being unified with one another.... Work on reconciling husbands and wives. . . . Resolve tensions in relationships in your body. . . . Give your people a vision of the harvest, and get them cooperating together toward a common goal. . . . Then forge into spiritual warfare." When we take seriously Jesus' command to love one another, his divine presence and power flow into the body. This dynamic drives the devil away. We don't need flashy campaigns and crusades to crush evil. We need to love one another in obedience to our Lord. This is the platform from which to do battle with powers of darkness.

DON'T GIVE THE DEVIL UNDUE CREDIT

One of the dangers in spiritual warfare is the tendency toward attribution—inaccurately ascribing demonic activity to non-supernatural problems. Not many people battle with direct demonic infestation. Most folks seem to wrestle with problems rooted primarily within themselves, and secondarily in the world and evil forces. Many people's struggles are related to basic psychological and emotional needs, or to body chemistry gone awry. If we are open to the possibility of enemy influence, and are prepared to respond to it, the Lord will help us discern accurately. But try to avoid the trap of inventing spirits that aren't really there. This does a disservice to the person seeking help and ultimately discredits the genuine work of deliverance.

WATCH FOR THE WIPE-OUTS

Paul admonishes us to "be alert and always keep on praying for all the saints" (Eph 6:18b). Let's practice this. Watch out for one another in the trench and cover a brother or sister with prayer.

There are times during warfare when everything seems out of whack. You feel dispirited and exhausted. Be extra cautious at these times. The devil plays dirty and hits us when our guard is down. Sometimes we are able to trace the source of the distress and pray about it. Other times it remains a mystery. Personally, Terri and I have found that some of these times indicate spiritual oppression which corresponds with a specific vulnerability or strategic ministry. Satanic forces try to strike us during the lows of life and drive us to despair. Their goal is to undermine our trust in the goodness of God.

Just as Paul learned to endure hardship and find grace through it (2 Cor 4:7-18), we must weather the blows. Picture, if you will, a surfer catching and riding a wave toward shore. Suddenly, the wave curls and devours him. The surfer finds himself scraping along the sandy bottom, mouth full of seaweed and sand, wondering in a panic whether he'll see the surface again. The best thing he can do is not panic, hold onto the board, and let the movement of the surf bring him back to the surface. In a similar fashion, the believer in crisis needs simply to hang on to what he knows of the faithfulness and goodness of God and wait to bob back above the waterline. I have found God to be faithful to bring me through troublesome times.

I was wallowing in a "black hole" one day, wondering how to find my way out, when the phone rang. It was Don Snow, a retired Army colonel and ministry board member: "Hey, White, what's going on with you? The Lord put you on my heart last night, and I can't stop praying. What's happening?" I told him. He said he would like to get several praying buddies together and drop in. I consented, though to be honest, I was wiped out and had little expectation that prayer would do any good. Five men gathered around me and began to pray. Nothing immediate or profound happened. The experience was comforting and therapeutic, though. It felt good. I went to bed that night with a quiet sense that I was in God's hands. I awoke in the morning, rested and renewed, ready for the next assignment. I have learned since that experience to ask for help, not to go it alone.

LEARN TO LIVE WITH THE MYSTERIES

There are times in this work when we are perplexed by unanswered questions and issues that boggle our minds. Some of these mysteries need to be left in a box labeled "God's Business." What is the relationship between God's sovereign will and man's free choice? How do angels respond to our prayers? How long and how much does a community need to pray before God sends his Spirit? Is there a theology of divine healing? For answers to these and a host of other questions, we can only keep seeking the mind of Jesus and be ready to receive whatever light he chooses to give.

Follow his lead, and leave the results in his hands. Guard yourself against frustration with God's hiddenness and temptation to charge him with disinterest or injustice. Just as Satan tried to make Job mistrust God, so he tempts us to lose confidence in our Master. Keep asking and searching for light and understanding, and accept what the Lord gives you. When answers seem insufficient, remind yourself that you have come this far by faith, and you'll need faith to finish the course.

LEARN THE SECRET OF PRAISE

Praise is an act of faith that affirms the character and redemptive power of God in all circumstances. If God truly dwells in the praises of his people, the regular practice of praise must be built into the lifestyle of the spiritual warrior. I used to feel weighed down by the burden of spiritual battles, but then I learned a secret. God waits for us to praise him so he can pour out his strength in us. Praise releases divine power to transform our perspective and our response to problems.

Consider an incident in the Old Testament that illustrates a right response by a righteous man named Jehoshaphat. The Moabites, Ammonites, and Meunites "came to make war on Jehoshaphat" (2 Chr 20:1). The king was predictably alarmed, yet "he resolved to inquire of the Lord, and he proclaimed a fast for all Judah" (v. 3). In a dismal situation, he turned to the Lord and prayed:

> Power and might are in your hand, and no one can withstand you.... If calamity comes upon us ... we will stand in your presence.... O Lord our God, will you not judge them? For we have no power to face this vast army that is attacking us. We do not know what to do, but our eyes are upon you. vs. 6, 9, 12

Jehoshaphat was letting God demonstrate his power amid human weakness. God loved the position this man took, and he honors it every time we take it! The king (Jehoshaphat) became a model of trust. He received counsel in a prophecy delivered by Jahaziel: "This is what the Lord says to you: 'Do not be afraid or discouraged because of this vast army. For the battle is not yours, but God's'" (v. 15b). And Jehoshaphat believed God's words.

Threatened by war, what did Jehoshaphat do next? The king led his people in worship, during which priests and musicians praised God "with very loud voice." The next morning it was time for battle. Instead of the urgent rustling of swords, spears, horses, and chariots, the camp was filled with praise. This man had the spiritual guts to appoint men to sing to the Lord and to praise him "for the splendor of his holiness" (v. 21). He reminded the people of the sufficiency of God and encouraged them to remain strong in faith: "Have faith in the Lord your God and you will be upheld; have faith in his prophets and you will be successful" (v. 20). As they began to praise God, he moved immediately to set ambushes against the enemy. The result: repudiation of the enemy (vs. 22-26), rejoicing in the camp, a celebration of victory (vs. 27, 28), a reverence for the Lord (v. 29), and rest for Israel (v. 30). What a remarkable picture of what happens when a leader trusts God.

As we face uncertain spiritual battles ahead—satanic darkness, secular humanism, the New Age phenomenon, and strongholds on the mission field—often we are not going to know what to do. Remember that the battle is the Lord's. Our job is to turn our gaze upon him, bow before him in worshipful trust, wait for his instruction, and wholeheartedly praise him. He will conquer the enemy and give rest to his people.

THE ARMY OF THE MOST HIGH

What a day to be on the Lord's side! He is raising an army. He is giving his soldiers their assignments. Some are spiritual warriors, some intercessors, others pastors, teachers, tentmakers, counselors, missionaries, and the list goes on. Everyone has a place on the Lord's side.

You may already know your role. Pray for greater power to fulfill it. For you who are uncertain of God's call on your life, ask God to show you your place in his work, and help you to fulfill it. We're in a battle for the eternal destiny of people. Let's take the battle seriously. Let's follow King Jehoshaphat's lead by placing the burden of the battle where it belongs, by joining with his band who led the army of Israel in singing.

Give thanks to the Lord, for his love endures forever.

Notes

Chapter One

1. Lewis, C.S., *The Screwtape Letters*, (NY: Macmillan Publishing Company, 1969), p. 38.

Chapter Two

1. Russell, D.S., *The Method of Jewish Apocalyptic*, (Philadelphia, PA: Westminster Press, 1964), pp. 237-38.

Chapter Three

1. Dickason, Fred, *Demon Possession and the Christian*, (Chicago, IL: Moody Press, 1987), p. 130.
2. Unger, Merrill, *What Demons Can Do to Saints*, (Chicago, IL: Moody Press, 1977), pp. 51-52.

Chapter Nine

1. Eastman, Dick, *Love on Its Knees*, (Old Tappan, NJ: Chosen Books, 1989), p. 65.